Collins Primary Maths
Pupil Book 1

5

Series Editor: Peter Clarke

Authors: Andrew Edmondson, Elizabeth Jurgensen,
Jeanette Mumford, Sandra Roberts

Contents

Shape and space:(2D)/ Reasoning and generalising about shapes/(position and direction)	To recognise properties of rectangles To solve mathematical problems or puzzles, recognise and explain patterns and relationships, generalise and predict. Suggest extensions asking "What if…?" To classify triangles (isosceles, equilateral, scalene), using criteria such as equal sides, equal angles, lines of symmetry To recognise positions: read and plot co-ordinates in the first quadrant	66–67, 68–69, 70–71, 72–73, 74–75, 76–77, 78–79
Measures: (area and perimeter) (length)/Making decisions/Problems involving measures (length)	To understand, measure and calculate perimeters of rectangles and regular polygons To measure and draw lines to the nearest millimetre To convert larger to smaller units (e.g. km to m, m to cm or mm) To choose and use appropriate number operations To solve problems, and appropriate ways of calculating: mental, mental with jottings, written methods, calculator	80–81, 82–83, 84–85, 86–87, 88–89, 90–91
Measures: (time)/Problems involving measures (time) Mental calculation strategies (+ and -)/Rapid recall of addition and subtraction facts	To use units of time: read the time on a 24-hour digital clock and use 24-hour clock notation, such as 19:53 To use known number facts and place value for mental addition and subtraction; add/subtract any pair of two-digit numbers, including crossing 100 To find differences by counting up through the next multiple of 10, 100 or 1000	92–93, 94–95, 96–97,
Pencil and paper procedures (+), Rapid recall of addition facts/Checking results of calculations Properties of numbers and number sequences	To use informal pencil and paper methods to support, record or explain additions To extend written methods to column addition of two whole integers less than 10 000 To recognise and extend number sequences formed by counting from any number in steps of constant size, extending beyond zero when counting back To know squares of numbers to at least 10×10 To find all the pairs of factors of any number up to 100	98–99, 100–101 106–107, 108–109, 110–111, 112–113
Reasoning and generalising about numbers	To solve mathematical problems or puzzles, recognise and explain patterns and relationships, generalise and predict. Suggest extensions asking "What if…?"	114–115

3

● Read and write whole numbers in figures and words, and know what each digit represents
● Use the vocabulary of comparing and ordering numbers
● Give one or more numbers lying between two given numbers

Get in order!

Practice

1 Write the **next** number.

    a 12 310   **b** 23 540   **c** 36 715

    d 45 126   **e** 17 822   **f** 28 207

    g 31 682   **h** 46 930   **i** 51 602

2 Choose two numbers to write out in words.

3 Put each set of numbers into **ascending** order.

    a

    b

    c

4 Put each set of numbers into **descending** order.

    a

    b

    c

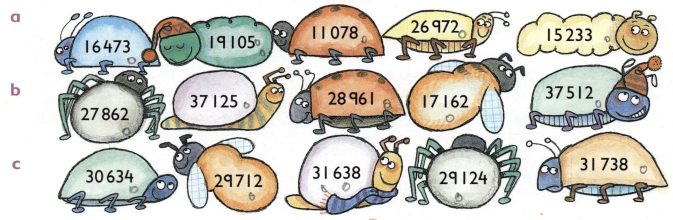

5 a Using the digits on the cards make eight five-digit numbers.

    b What is the smallest number you can make?

    c What is the largest number you can make?

    d Write down four numbers that come between 23 756 and 35 627.

4

Refresher

1 Write out these numbers filling in the boxes.

a 4523   4524   ☐   4526   ☐   4528   4529   ☐   ☐   4532

b 6174   ☐   6176   6177   ☐   ☐   6180   ☐   6182   ☐

c 7006   ☐   7008   ☐   ☐   7011   ☐   7013   ☐

d 9338   ☐   ☐   9341   ☐   9343   ☐   ☐   9346   ☐

e 8299   ☐   8301   ☐   ☐   8304   ☐   8306   ☐   8308

2 Put each set of numbers in order, smallest to largest.
Write the numbers in red in words.

a 1862   3496   1748   2956   2832   b 5812   5630   5047   5578   5200

c 6302   6354   3687   3612   3318   d 1985   9143   1830   8144   9102

3 Write one number that comes between these two numbers.

a 1200   ☐   2310   b 3654   ☐   4860

c 4002   ☐   5100   d 5812   ☐   6584

Challenge

Work in twos, threes or fours.

Play again with these numbers.

You need:
- paper
- pencil

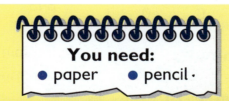

What to do

1 Write one of these numbers at the top of your paper.
Each of you must choose a different number.
The target number is 57 000.   56 952   56 938   56 945   56 963

2 Next to the number you have written, write the number that comes next.
Then give your paper to the player sitting next to you.

3 On the paper you have received, write the next number.
Give your paper to the next player.

4 Keep going until somebody writes 57 000. They are the winner.

67 462   67 455   67 428   67 439 – Play again using these
numbers. The target number is 67 500

Round them!

Practice

1 Copy the table into your book.
   Round these numbers to the nearest
   multiple of 10 and 100.
   The first one has been done for you.

Number	Nearest multiple of 10	Nearest multiple of 100
761	760	800
a 264		
b 351		
c 748		
d 426		
e 534		
f 1237		
g 6004		
h 3850		
i 7963		
j 8507		

2 Multiply these numbers by 10 and by
   100. Write your answers as
   calculations.

Tth	Th	H	T	U
			7	2
		7	2	0
	7	2	0	0

Example

72

$72 \times 10 = 720$

$72 \times 100 = 7200$

a 45   b 62
c 38   d 91
e 70   f 642
g 845   h 963
i 752   j 809

k Explain what happens when numbers
   are multiplied by 10 or 100.

3 Divide these numbers by 10 and by 100.
   Write your answers as calculations.

Tth	Th	H	T	U
	5	1	0	0
		5	1	0
			5	1

Example

5100

$5100 \div 10 = 510$

$5100 \div 100 = 51$

a 3200   b 7500   c 2900
d 8300   e 5000   f 84 000
g 29 000   h 84 700   i 61 900

j Explain what happens when numbers
   are divided by 10 or 100.

Refresher

Example
64→60

1 Round these numbers to the nearest multiple of 10.

a 48	b 32	c 18	d 59	e 65
f 77	g 82	h 61	i 93	j 76

Example
$8 \times 10 = 80$

2 Multiply these numbers by 10.

a 7	b 9	c 5	d 29	e 64
f 37	g 56	h 73	i 83	j 152

3 Divide these numbers by 10.

a 80	b 40	c 50	d 320	e 460
f 910	g 570	h 650	i 120	j 3500

Challenge

You need:

- 10 counters 5 of one colour, 5 of another
- a die labelled ×10, ×10, ×100, ÷10, ÷100, ÷100
- paper and pencil

What to do

Play the game with a partner.

1 Choose a number from the board. Throw the die. Carry out the operation on your number and write the answer.

2 Your partner then chooses their number and does the same.

3 The player with the highest answer covers their chosen number with one of their counters.

4 The winner is the first player to have three counters in a row.

9100	1700	6300	5600
7600	200	300	2200
4800	500	100	9900
800	8100	7200	1000

Key it in

Practice

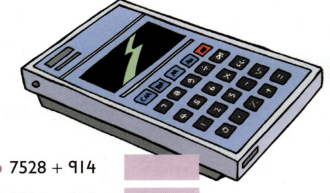

1 Use the calculator to work out these calculations. Enter the numbers carefully!

a 4823 + 684

b 7528 + 914

c 8473 + 654

d 3819 + 829

e 2674 + 2941

f 7458 − 657

g 8631 − 752

h 6831 − 458

i 7635 − 1579

j 4197 − 2067

k 49 × 37

l 98 × 62

m 157 × 36

n 261 × 75

o 452 × 103

p 5724 ÷ 36

q 14 736 ÷ 48

r 54 610 ÷ 86

s 24 388 ÷ 91

t 21 424 ÷ 52

Now check your answers with a friend.

2

Calculator cricket

What to do

Play with a partner.
1 One player chooses a five-digit number, for example 43 578, enters it into the calculator and writes it down.
2 The player then underlines one of the digits.
3 The other player has to say the subtraction calculation to make that digit zero.
4 The first player then enters the calculation into the calculator to check the result.

You need:
● one calculator between you

Refresher

1 Use the calculator to work out these calculations.
Enter the numbers carefully!

a 485 + 67

b 279 + 81

c 578 + 391

d 570 + 294

e 617 + 271

f 751 − 68

g 593 − 81

h 642 − 291

i 384 − 173

j 759 − 218

k 16 × 43

l 36 × 21

m 26 × 13

n 17 × 33

o 22 × 38

p 216 ÷ 8

q 306 ÷ 9

r 294 ÷ 7

s 318 ÷ 6

t 592 ÷ 8

Calculator cricket

2

What to do

Play with a partner.
1 One player chooses a **four**-digit
   number, for example 6532, enters it
   into the calculator and writes it down.
2 The player then underlines one of the digits.
3 The other player has to say the subtraction
   calculation to make that digit zero.
4 The first player then enters the calculation
   into the calculator to check the result.

You need:
● one calculator
  between you

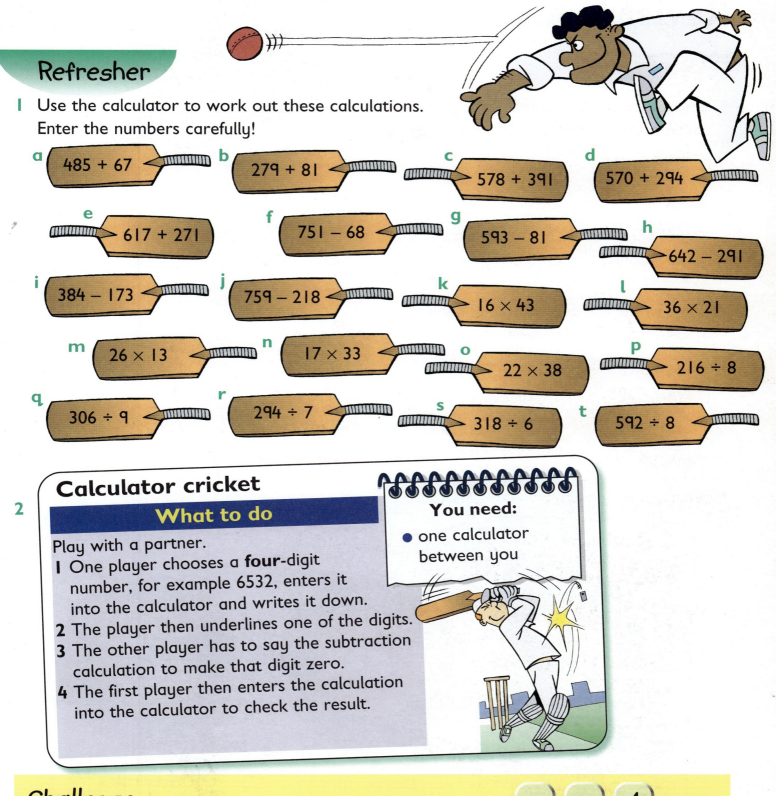

Challenge

1 Can you make all the numbers to 20 on your calculator?
   You are only allowed to press these keys:

9

Revising multiplication facts

Practice

1 Copy and complete.

a
7 × 6 =
4 × 9 =
8 × 3 =
6 × 6 =
9 × 5 =

b
3 × 9 =
6 × 9 =
7 × 8 =
8 × 6 =
4 × 1 =

c
× 6 = 42
× 8 = 40
× ⎕ = 32
× ⎕ = 24
× ⎕ = 49

2 Some of the answers to the multiplication facts are incorrect.
Find the incorrect calculations and write them correctly.

Example
7 × 7 = 14 ✗
7 × 7 = 49

a 3 × 8 = 24
b 4 × 6 = 23
c 5 × 8 = 35
d 7 × 4 = 27
e 9 × 4 = 34
f 3 × 7 = 27
g 9 × 6 = 56
h 10 × 7 = 70
i 7 × 7 = 47
j 8 × 9 = 72
k 3 × 6 = 15
l 8 × 8 = 62
m 3 × 9 = 29
n 4 × 4 = 12
o 5 × 6 = 30

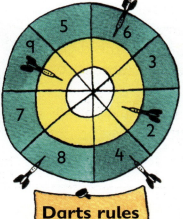

3 Calculate the score for each dart thrown.

a
Example
3 × 7 = 21

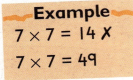

Numbers: 2, 8, 3, 6, 9, 5, 4, 7

Darts rules
White: ×4
Yellow ×7
Green: ×9

b
Numbers: 5, 6, 9, 3, 7, 2, 8, 4

Darts rules
White: ×6
Yellow: ×3
Green: ×8

c
Numbers: 4, 5, 1, 6, 2, 8, 9, 3

Darts rules
White: ×5
Yellow: ×2
Green: ×7

Refresher

Write a multiplication fact for each number going into the machine. Write the answer.

a

| 7 |
| 3 |
| 6 |
| 4 |
| 8 |

 ×5

b

| 6 |
| 9 |
| 4 |
| 7 |
| 8 |

 ×4

c

| 5 |
| 2 |
| 9 |
| 8 |
| 7 |

 ×3

d

| 3 |
| 7 |
| 9 |
| 4 |
| 6 |

 ×9

e

| 7 |
| 2 |
| 6 |
| 3 |
| 8 |

 ×2

f

| 9 |
| 4 |
| 10 |
| 6 |
| 7 |

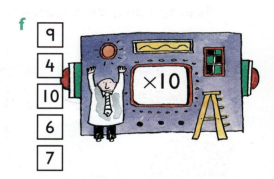 ×10

Challenge

1 Copy and complete each of these grids.

a

×	4	8	1	10
3				
8				
6				
9				
5				
1				
7				

b

×		4	2			8
			6	21		
5	45			5	30	
						56

c

×		3		4	
2	12				14
			48	24	
		27			
0					

Revising division facts

Practice

1 Each bowling ball will only hit pins that are multiples of it.
Find the multiples and write a multiplication and division fact for each.

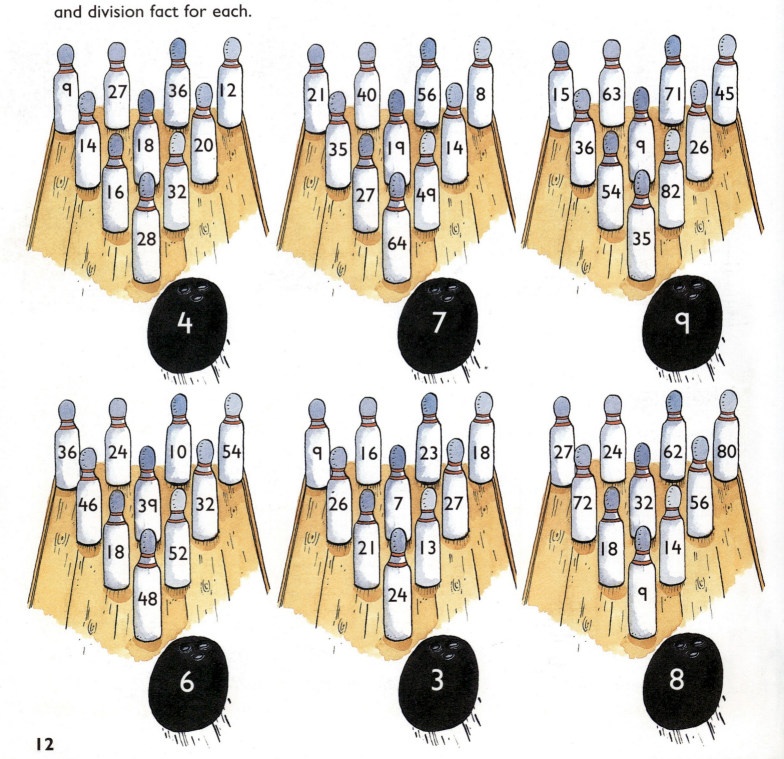

Refresher

1 Write a division fact for each number coming out of the machine. Write the answer.

a
| 24 |
| 16 |
| 40 |
| 32 |
| 8 |

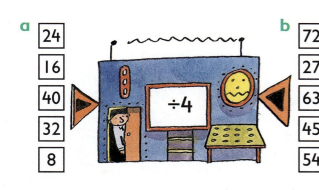

b
| 72 |
| 27 |
| 63 |
| 45 |
| 54 |

c
| 12 |
| 18 |
| 14 |
| 6 |
| 16 |

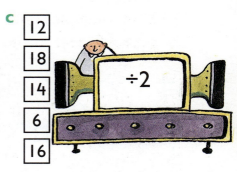

d
| 35 |
| 25 |
| 30 |
| 40 |
| 45 |

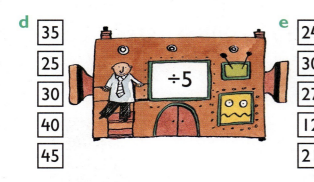

e
| 24 |
| 30 |
| 27 |
| 12 |
| 21 |

f
| 9 |
| 4 |
| 6 |
| 8 |
| 7 |

Challenge

Copy and complete these calculations.

1 a $(32 \div 8) \times 4 = \square$
   b $(72 \div 9) \times 3 = \square$
   c $(15 \div 3) \times 6 = \square$
   d $(27 \div 3) \times 9 = \square$
   e $(24 \div 4) \times 7 = \square$
   f $(56 \div 7) \times 8 = \square$
   g $(36 \div 6) \times 6 = \square$
   h $(100 \div 10) \times 0 = \square$

2 a $(32 \div \square) \times 3 = 24$
   b $(48 \div \square) \times 5 = 30$
   c $(64 \div \square) \times 7 = 56$
   d $(12 \div \square) \times 9 = 36$
   e $(\square \div 5) \times 6 = 24$
   f $(\square \div 3) \times 3 = 21$
   g $(\square \div 2) \times 8 = 64$
   h $(\square \div 1) \times 9 = 63$

3 a $(35 \div 5) \times \square = 28$
   b $(42 \div 6) \times \square = 28$
   c $(28 \div 4) \times \square = 28$
   d $(63 \div 7) \times \square = 45$
   e $(81 \div 9) \times \square = 54$
   f $(8 \div 1) \times \square = 56$
   g $(49 \div 7) \times \square = 42$
   h $(20 \div 5) \times \square = 36$

Multiplication methods

Practice

1 Approximate the answer to each calculation.

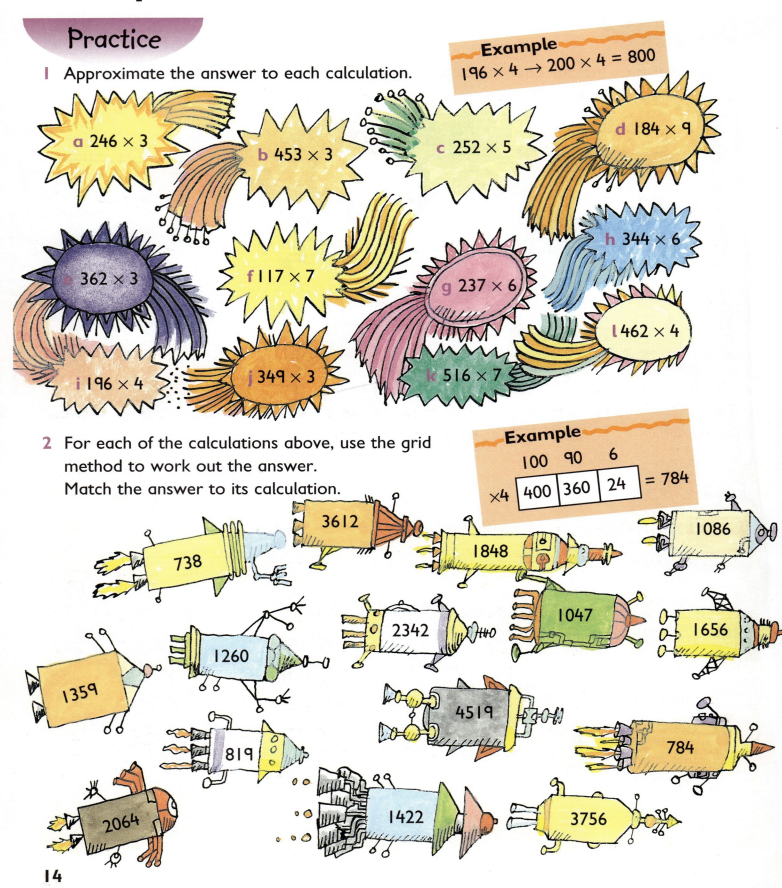

a 246 × 3

b 453 × 3

c 252 × 5

d 184 × 9

e 362 × 3

f 117 × 7

g 237 × 6

h 344 × 6

i 196 × 4

j 349 × 3

k 516 × 7

l 462 × 4

2 For each of the calculations above, use the grid method to work out the answer.
Match the answer to its calculation.

Example

	100	90	6	
×4	400	360	24	= 784

3612

738

1848

1086

2342

1047

1656

1260

1359

4519

784

819

2064

1422

3756

14

Refresher

1 Copy and complete. Write the multiples of 10 which each number is **between**.
Circle which multiple of 10 the number is closest to.

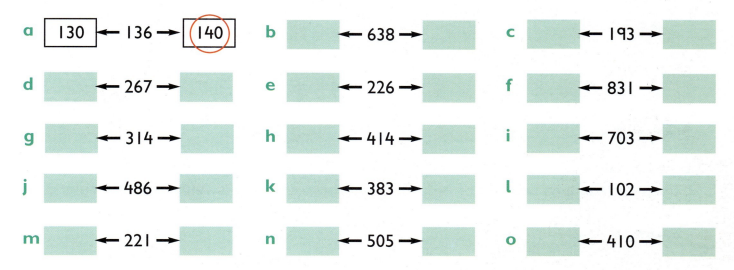

a [130] ← 136 → (140)   b [ ] ← 638 → [ ]   c [ ] ← 193 → [ ]

d [ ] ← 267 → [ ]   e [ ] ← 226 → [ ]   f [ ] ← 831 → [ ]

g [ ] ← 314 → [ ]   h [ ] ← 414 → [ ]   i [ ] ← 703 → [ ]

j [ ] ← 486 → [ ]   k [ ] ← 383 → [ ]   l [ ] ← 102 → [ ]

m [ ] ← 221 → [ ]   n [ ] ← 505 → [ ]   o [ ] ← 410 → [ ]

2 For each of the numbers above, write the multiples of 100 which each number is between.
Circle which multiple of 100 the number is closest to.

Challenge

In each set of calculations one calculation is the odd one out.
Find the odd one out and explain your reasons.

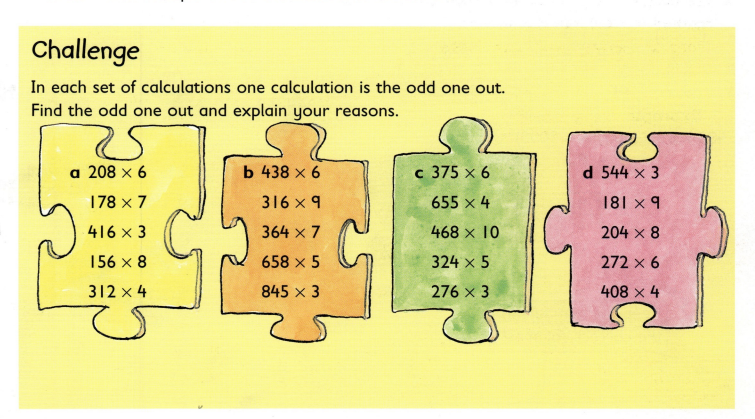

a 208 × 6
178 × 7
416 × 3
156 × 8
312 × 4

b 438 × 6
316 × 9
364 × 7
658 × 5
845 × 3

c 375 × 6
655 × 4
468 × 10
324 × 5
276 × 3

d 544 × 3
181 × 9
204 × 8
272 × 6
408 × 4

Multiplication methods

Practice

1 Write multiplication facts for each bag.

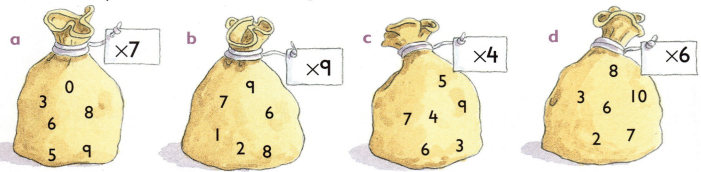

2 Look at the calculations below. Approximate your answer first.
   Choose a standard method of recording to work out the answer to each calculation.

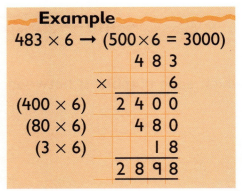

or

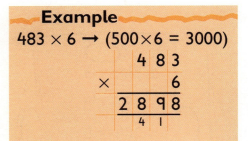

Remember

Keep the numbers in the correct columns!

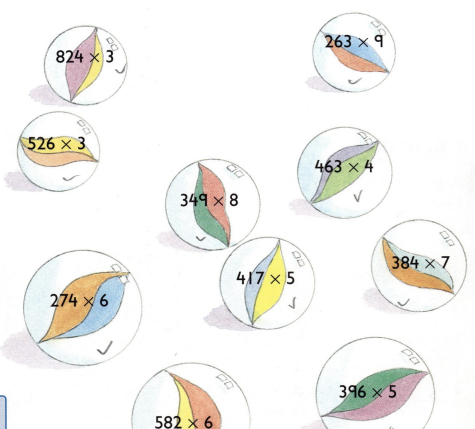

16

Refresher

Partition each of these calculations. The first one has been done for you.

a 264 × 6

b 435 × 9

Example

264 × 6 = (200 × 6) + (60 × 6) + (4 × 6)
= 1200 + 360 + 24
= 1584

c 273 × 4

d 539 × 6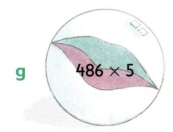

e 376 × 7

f 484 × 8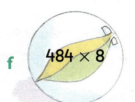

h 463 × 4

i 278 × 3

g 486 × 5

j 326 × 3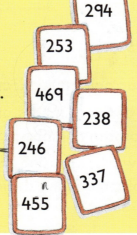

Challenge

1 Copy the centre grid.

2 Multiply the numbers on the left by a number on the right.

3 Can you find the correct calculations? Write the calculation in the correct square on the grid.

294

253

469

238

246

337

455

✓	✓	✓
4221	2277	1176
✓	✓	✓
2359	2696	2352
✓	✓	✓
1771	1428	1820

9

7

4

8

6

Multiplying decimals

Practice

The function machines partition numbers into whole numbers and decimal numbers.

1 Write the number as it will come out of the machine.

a

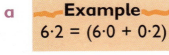

Example
6·2 = (6·0 + 0·2)

4·3
2·7
6·8
7·5
3·1

b

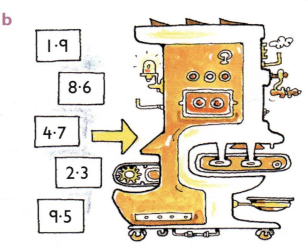

1·9
8·6
4·7
2·3
9·5

c

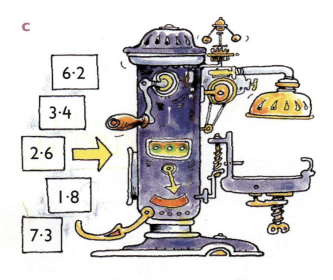

6·2
3·4
2·6
1·8
7·3

d

5·4
4·1
3·8
6·6
5·3

2 You need a 1–6 die.

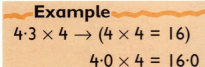

Example

4·3 × 4 → (4 × 4 = 16)

4·0 × 4 = 16·0

0·3 × 4 = 1·2

——————
17·2
——————

Write your own multiplication calculations.

For each of the numbers above roll the die to give you the number to multiply by.

Set your work out using the standard method of multiplying decimals.

Refresher

1 Copy and complete. Write the whole numbers that each decimal number is **between**. Circle the whole number which the decimal number is closest to. The first one is done for you.

a [(3)] ← 3·4 → [4]   b ⬚ ← 2·4 → ⬚   c ⬚ ← 9·7 → ⬚

d ⬚ ← 4·7 → ⬚   e ⬚ ← 3·8 → ⬚   f ⬚ ← 4·0 → ⬚

g ⬚ ← 8·5 → ⬚   h ⬚ ← 5·5 → ⬚   i ⬚ ← 2·9 → ⬚

j ⬚ ← 9·2 → ⬚   k ⬚ ← 4·1 → ⬚   l ⬚ ← 7·3 → ⬚

m ⬚ ← 1·6 → ⬚   n ⬚ ← 6·9 → ⬚   o ⬚ ← 8·2 → ⬚

Challenge

1 For each set of calculations decide which gives the largest answer.

2 Write your approximations.

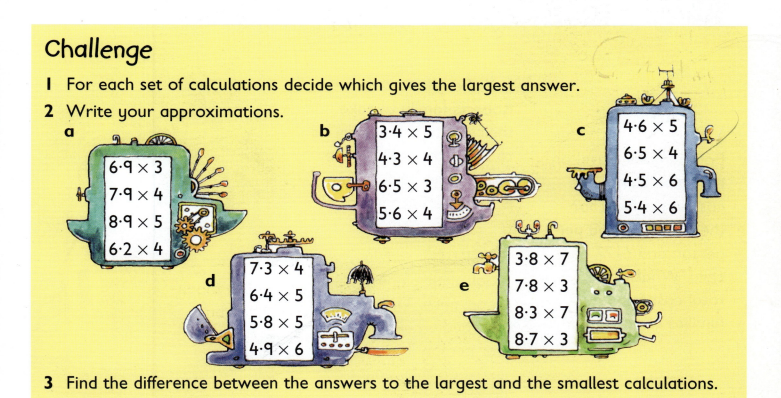

a
6·9 × 3
7·9 × 4
8·9 × 5
6·2 × 4

b
3·4 × 5
4·3 × 4
6·5 × 3
5·6 × 4

c
4·6 × 5
6·5 × 4
4·5 × 6
5·4 × 6

d
7·3 × 4
6·4 × 5
5·8 × 5
4·9 × 6

e
3·8 × 7
7·8 × 3
8·3 × 7
8·7 × 3

3 Find the difference between the answers to the largest and the smallest calculations.

Solving word problems

Practice

1 Read the word problems. Choose an appropriate method of calculating your answers.

The Roberts family

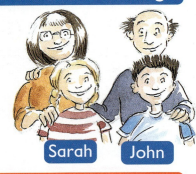

Sarah   John

The Kruger family

Joanne   James
Simone   Bobby

a A cab to the airport will cost the Kruger family £40. The train costs £9·50 for adults and £6 for children. Which is the cheaper option and by how much?

b The Roberts family drive to the airport. Parking costs £5·80 per day for the first seven days and £4·60 per day after that. How much does car parking cost for their ten-day holiday?

c The Kruger family need to purchase travel insurance. Family cover costs £235. Separate cover costs £58 for adults and £34 for children. Which cover will cost the family the least and by how much?

d Is it cheaper for the Roberts family to take their car to the airport or to catch the train to the airport and back? What is the difference in price?

e Both families travel on the same plane. The cost of the flight for the adults is £368 per person and £177 per child. What is the total cost for both families together?

f The Kruger family book their plane seats in advance. They are charged an extra £26 per person. How much extra do they pay altogether?

Refresher

Write the calculation needed to answer each of these problems.

a The Roberts family are going on holiday in six weeks' time. How many days is that?

~**Example**~
6 × 7 = 42

b The Kruger family are going on holiday for four weeks. How many days will they be away for?

c Sarah and John have saved a total of £28 between them. How much have they saved each?

d Joanne gets £5 pocket money per week. She has saved up for nine weeks. How much money does she have?

e Simone gets £7 for washing the family car. She has saved a total of £56. How many times has she washed the car?

f There are four people in the Roberts family. Mum buys one bottle of sunscreen per person. Each bottle costs £6. What is the total cost?

Challenge

1 Use the information on the opposite page to plan a 7 day holiday for the Patel family (2 adults, 3 children). They have a budget of £2000. Find the cheapest options to enable them to stick to their budget.

a Draw up a price list.

Cab:.........
Train:.........
Parking:.........
Insurance:.........
Accommodation:.........
Flights:.........

b Find the cheapest transport to and from the airport.

c Find the cost of flights.

d Prepare a final invoice listing the costs of each item and the final price.

INVOICE
Transport:.........
Flights:.........
Insurance:.........
Accommodation:.........
Total:.........

Doubles and halves

Practice

1 Find the multiples of 10. Double them. Record your answer in two different ways.

Example
130 + 130 = 260
130 × 2 = 260

2 Find the multiples of 20. Halve them. Record your answer in two different ways.

Example
260 ÷ 2 = 130
½ × 260 = 130

3 Copy and complete the diagrams to show that halving is the inverse of doubling.

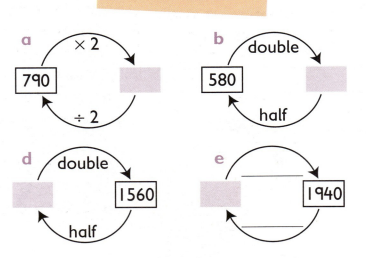

a × 2
790 [ ]
÷ 2

b double
580 [ ]
half

c × 2
[ ] 1380
÷ 2

d double
[ ] 1560
half

e
[ ] 1940

f
370 [ ]

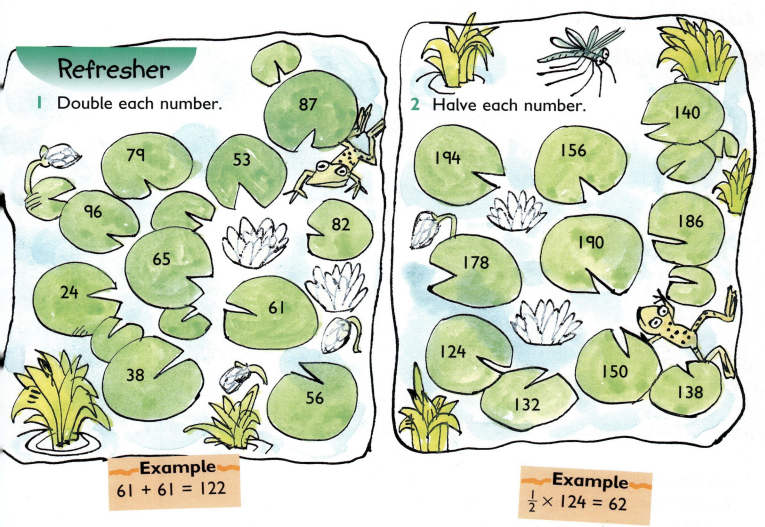

Refresher

1 Double each number.

87

79

53

96

82

65

24

61

38

56

2 Halve each number.

140

194

156

186

190

178

124

150

132

138

Example
61 + 61 = 122

Example
$\frac{1}{2} \times 124 = 62$

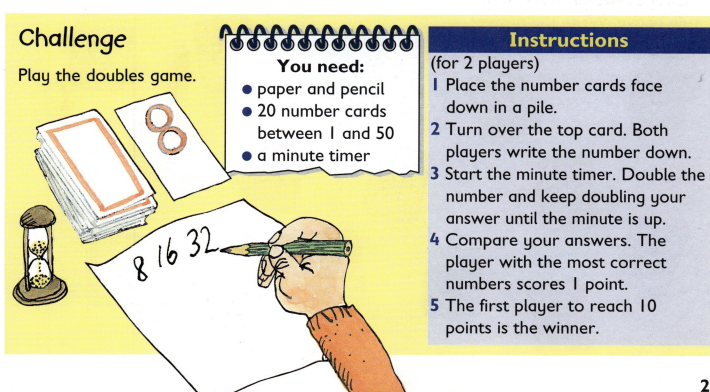

Challenge

Play the doubles game.

You need:
- paper and pencil
- 20 number cards between 1 and 50
- a minute timer

8 16 32

Instructions

(for 2 players)

1 Place the number cards face down in a pile.
2 Turn over the top card. Both players write the number down.
3 Start the minute timer. Double the number and keep doubling your answer until the minute is up.
4 Compare your answers. The player with the most correct numbers scores 1 point.
5 The first player to reach 10 points is the winner.

Quick fifty

Practice

RULE:
TO ×50
first
× 100
then
÷2

1 Use the rule shown on the notebook to calculate the answers to these.

a 12 × 50

Example
(12 × 100) ÷ 2 = 1200 ÷ 2 = 600

b 27 × 50

c 33 × 50

d 48 × 50

e 16 × 50

f 29 × 50

g 36 × 50

h 15 × 50

i 44 × 50

j 50 × 50

Bonus

Try these:

a 54 × 50

b 62 × 50

c 58 × 50

d 55 × 50

e 66 × 50

2 Try to work out the answers to these in your head. Choose 10 numbers. Multiply them by 50 using the rule above. Write the answer.

Refresher

1 Multiply the number shown on the calculator display by 100. Write the new number.

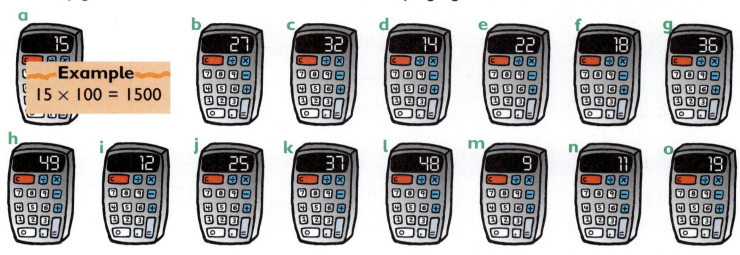

a 15

Example
15 × 100 = 1500

b 27 c 32 d 14 e 22 f 18 g 36

h 49 i 12 j 25 k 37 l 48 m 9 n 11 o 19

Challenge

This is a doubling and halving pattern for you to try.
It works when one of the numbers you are multiplying ends in 5.

What to do
- Double the number that ends in 5.
- Halve the other number.
- What is the answer?

Try some yourself!
Multiply 2 numbers together

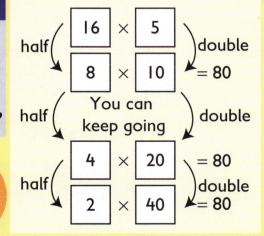

half (16 × 5) double
8 × 10 = 80

half (You can keep going) double
4 × 20 = 80

half (2 × 40) double = 80

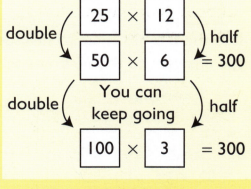

double (25 × 12) half
50 × 6 = 300

double (You can keep going) half
100 × 3 = 300

1 Choose one number that ends in 5 and one other number. Complete ten calculations.

26   15   35   5   45
48
53   36   27   49
33   57   25

Doubling multiplication facts

Practice

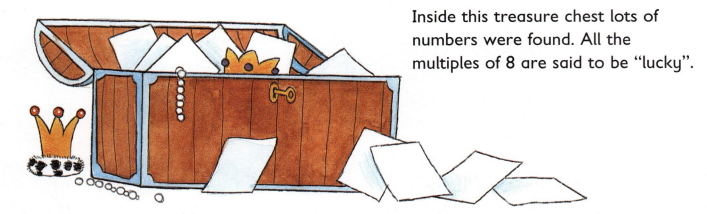

Inside this treasure chest lots of numbers were found. All the multiples of 8 are said to be "lucky".

1 Find the multiples of 8.
2 Write out the multiplication fact for 8 that matches the number card.

Example
$2 \times 8 = 16$

32   18   48   74   ~~16~~   56   46   80

24   64   26   52   8   72   40

3 Use the 8 times table to help you find the answers to the 16 times table.

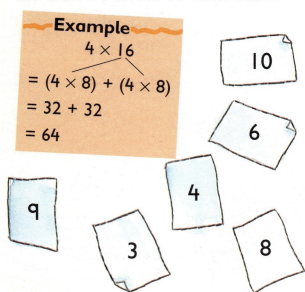

Example
$$4 \times 16$$
$$= (4 \times 8) + (4 \times 8)$$
$$= 32 + 32$$
$$= 64$$

10   6   9   4   3   8

4 Find the answer to each number fact for 16 by multiplying by 8 then doubling your answer.

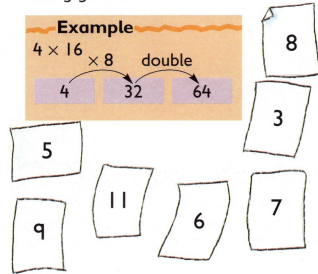

Example
4×16
$\times 8$ double

| 4 | 32 | 64 |

8   5   3   9   11   6   7

Refresher

Inside the treasure chest lots of numbers were found. All multiples of 4 are said to be "lucky".

1 Find all the multiples of 4.

2 Write out the multiplication fact for 4 that matches the number card.

Example
$2 \times 4 = 8$

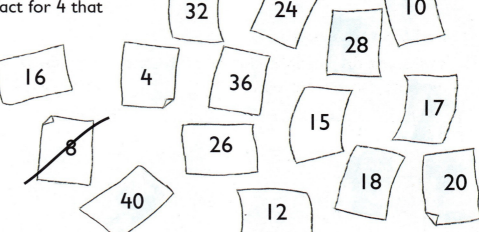

32   24   10
28
16   4   36
17
15
26
8
18   20
40   12

Challenge

1 How quickly can you work out the answers to the 16 times table? Work with a partner.

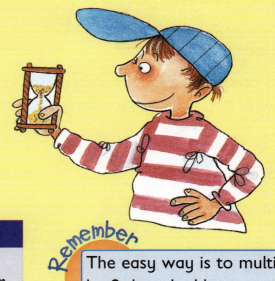

You need:
● a 12-sided die

What to do
● Roll the die.
● Multiply the number landed on by 16.

Remember
The easy way is to multiply by 8 then double.

Finding sixths

Practice

1 Find out how many pieces of fruit there are in each part of the box. Find the answer by finding one third of the total first and then halving.

> **Example**
> One third of 300 is 100.
> One half of 100 is 50.
> One sixth of 300 is 50.

a Total pieces of fruit
300

b Total pieces of fruit
120

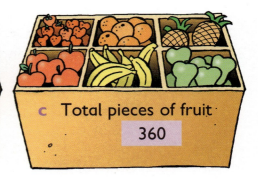

c Total pieces of fruit
360

d Total pieces of fruit
180

e Total pieces of fruit
240

f Total pieces of fruit
420

2 Find one sixth of each number. Find one third of the number first then halve it to get your answer.

a $\frac{1}{6} \times 48$

one third   half

b $\frac{1}{6} \times 24$

one third   half

c $\frac{1}{6} \times 72$

one third   half

d $\frac{1}{6} \times 540$

one third $\frac{1}{2}$

e $\frac{1}{6} \times 660$

$\frac{1}{3}$ $\frac{1}{2}$

f $\frac{1}{6} \times 36$

$\frac{1}{3}$ $\frac{1}{2}$

Refresher

1 Divide each bag of fruit by 3. How many will each person get? Write a division fact.

a 18
b 24
c 6
d 12
e 30
f 15

2 Divide each bag of fruit by 6. How many will each person get? Write a division fact.

a 24
b 30
c 36
d 48
e 12
f 54

Challenge

1 Copy and complete each number web.
Find one sixth of each number shown.

Remember

Find one third first then halve it to get your answer.

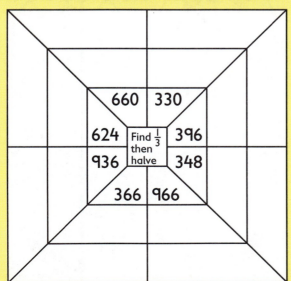

660 330
624 | Find ⅓ then halve | 396
936 | 348
366 966

630
372 | Find ⅓ then halve | 942
324 | 648
960 918

29

What's left?

Practice

1 Look at the cakes. Describe the pieces left in two ways, as a mixed number and an improper fraction.

a

b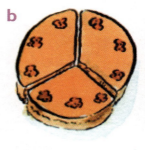

c

d

e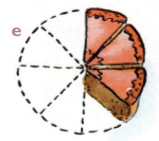

f

g

h

Refresher

1   What fraction of each pizza is left?

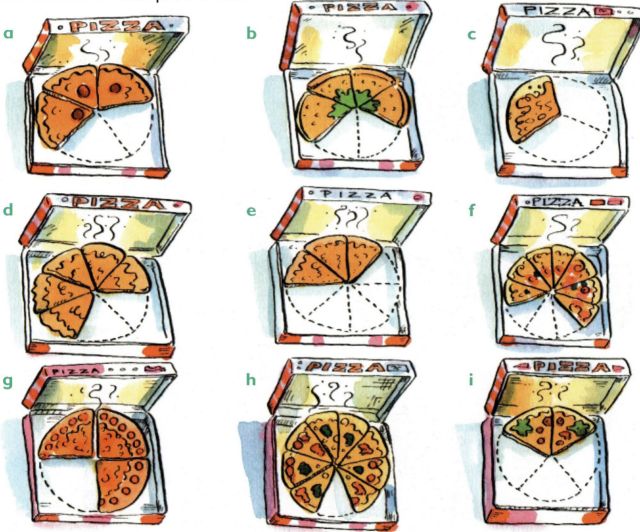

2   Now write each fraction in words.

> **Example**
>
> $\frac{2}{3}$ = two thirds

Challenge

Look at the improper fractions and mixed numbers in the Practice section. Can you find a way to change an improper fraction into a mixed number using division?

Are they equal?

Practice

1 Find the equivalent fractions.

Example

$\frac{1}{2} = \frac{2}{4} = \ldots$

$\frac{6}{12}$ $\frac{4}{8}$ $\frac{1}{2}$ $\frac{3}{6}$

$\frac{2}{4}$ $\frac{5}{8}$

$\frac{9}{12}$ $\frac{5}{10}$

$\frac{3}{4}$ $\frac{7}{14}$ $\frac{6}{8}$ $\frac{6}{9}$

2 Find the equivalent fractions for a third.

a    b 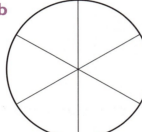   c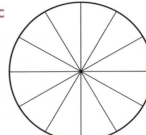

What patterns do you see in the equivalent fractions for a third?

3 Find the equivalent fractions for a fifth.

a 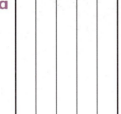   b 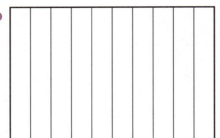   c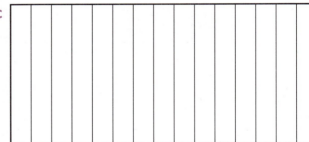

What patterns do you see in the equivalent fractions for a fifth?

4 Find the equivalent fractions for a tenth.

a 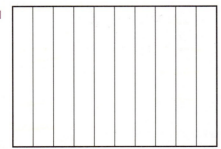   b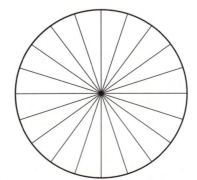

What patterns do you see in the equivalent fractions for a tenth?

Refresher

1 How many fractions would need to be shaded to make a half?

a 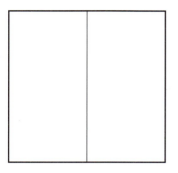   b 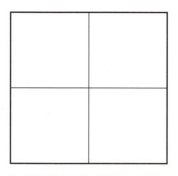   c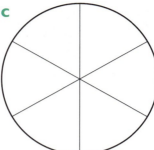

d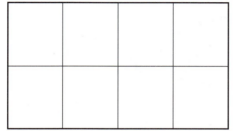

2 How many fractions would need to be shaded to make a quarter?

a 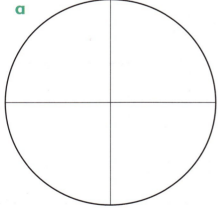   b 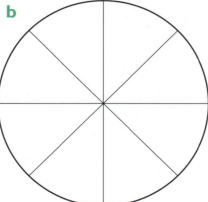   c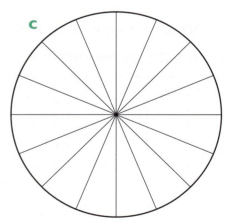

Challenge

What fractions are equivalent to $\frac{1}{6}$? What is the pattern? Investigate other equivalent fractions.

Example

$\frac{1}{6} = \frac{2}{12} = \ldots$

Tenths and hundredths

Practice

What fraction of each grid has been shaded? Describe it as tenths and hundredths.

a 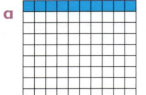   b    c 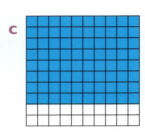   d 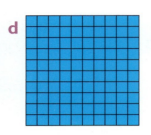   e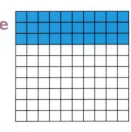

f 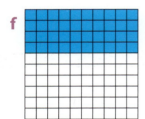   g    h 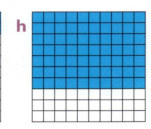   i 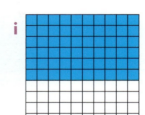   j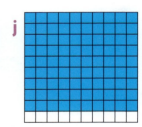

Colour the hundredths!

You need:
- a 10 × 10 grid each
- 1 die labelled $\frac{10}{100}$, $\frac{20}{100}$, $\frac{1}{10}$, $\frac{2}{10}$, M, D
- a coloured pencil each

What to do

(for 2 to 3 players)
1 Take it in turns to throw the die.
2 Colour in the fraction shown on the die.
3 If you throw M you miss a turn.
4 If you throw D you throw again and double your score.
5 The winner is the first player to colour all of their grid.

Refresher

1 What fraction of each stick has been shaded? Describe it as tenths.

a $\frac{7}{10}$

b

c

d

e

f

g

h

i

j

Challenge

1 Investigate the equivalence between tenths, hundredths and twentieths.

a $\frac{1}{10} = \frac{10}{100} = \frac{?}{20}$

b $\frac{2}{10} = \frac{?}{100} = \frac{?}{20}$

c $\frac{3}{10} = \frac{?}{100} = \frac{?}{20}$

d $\frac{4}{10} = \frac{?}{100} = \frac{?}{20}$

e $\frac{5}{10} = \frac{?}{100} = \frac{?}{20}$

f $\frac{6}{10} = \frac{?}{100} = \frac{?}{20}$

g $\frac{7}{10} = \frac{?}{100} = \frac{?}{20}$

h $\frac{8}{10} = \frac{?}{100} = \frac{?}{20}$

i $\frac{9}{10} = \frac{?}{100} = \frac{?}{20}$

j $\frac{10}{10} = \frac{?}{100} = \frac{?}{20}$

2 What pattern do you see?

● Know what each digit represents in a number with up to two decimal places
● Use decimal notation for tenths and hundredths

Au 4, 4

Tent tenths

Practice

1 These tents have been put up in the wrong order. What order should they be in?

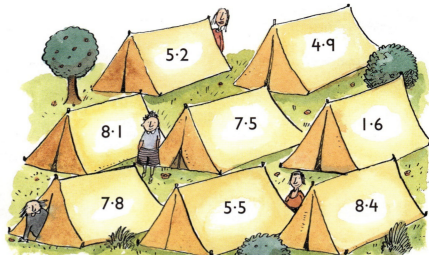

Example

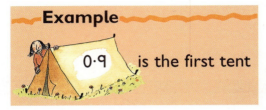

0·9 is the first tent

2 What tent should be next to these?

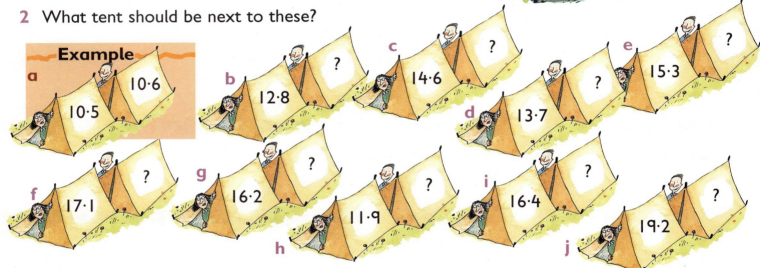

Example

a 10·5 10·6

b 12·8 ?

c 14·6 ?

d 13·7 ?

e 15·3 ?

f 17·1 ?

g 16·2 ?

h 11·9 ?

i 16·4 ?

j 19·2 ?

3 What is one tent that will come between these?

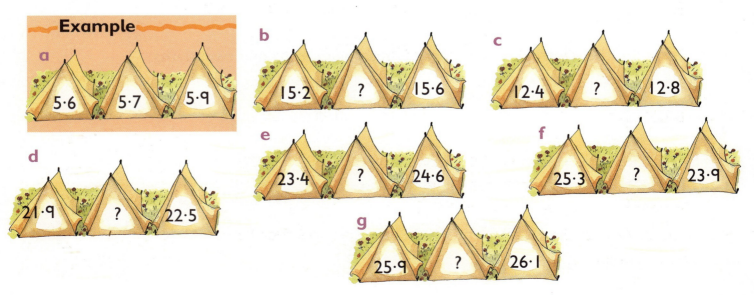

Example

a 5·6 5·7 5·9

b 15·2 ? 15·6

c 12·4 ? 12·8

d 21·9 ? 22·5

e 23·4 ? 24·6

f 25·3 ? 23·9

g 25·9 ? 26·1

Refresher

1 Write the tenths from 0 to 1 as decimal fractions.

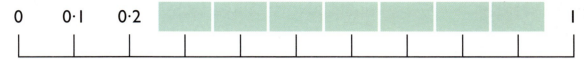

0   0·1   0·2   1

2 Put these decimal fractions in order. Use the number line to help you.

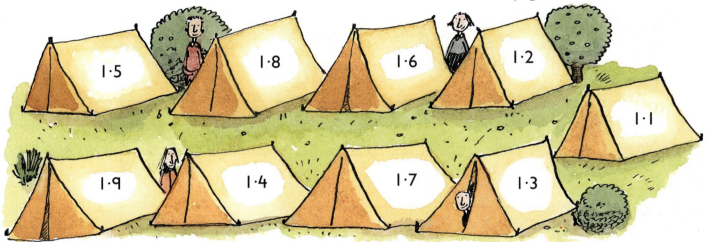

1·5   1·8   1·6   1·2   1·1   1·9   1·4   1·7   1·3

3 Copy out the sequences filling in the missing numbers

a	2·3	2·4		2·6		2·8		3	3·1	3·2
b	4·6		4·8		5		5·2		5·4	
c	3·8		4		4·2	4·3			4·6	
d	5·5		5·7		5·9		6·1	6·2		
e	6·7			7	7·1			7·4		7·6

Challenge

1 Use these digits and make 24 two-digit numbers to one decimal place as you can, for example 42·6.
Put them in order from smallest to largest.

2 Choose two of the numbers. Write all the numbers that come between them.

All in order

Practice

1 Copy out the number lines filling in the missing numbers. The first one is done for you.

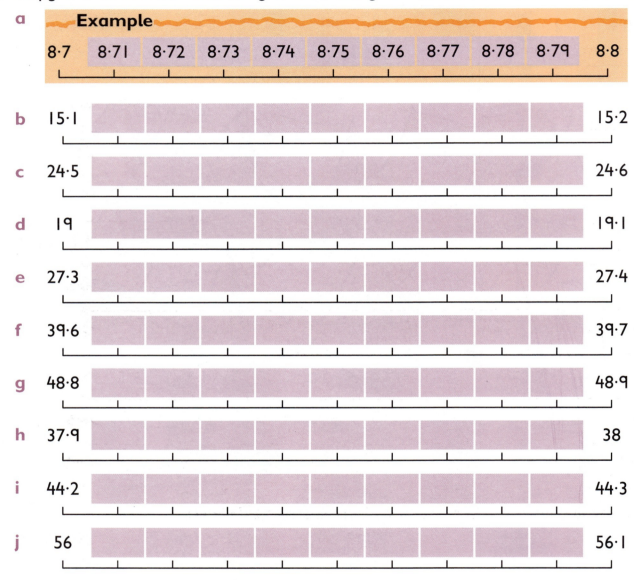

a **Example**

| 8·7 | 8·71 | 8·72 | 8·73 | 8·74 | 8·75 | 8·76 | 8·77 | 8·78 | 8·79 | 8·8 |

b 15·1 ___ 15·2

c 24·5 ___ 24·6

d 19 ___ 19·1

e 27·3 ___ 27·4

f 39·6 ___ 39·7

g 48·8 ___ 48·9

h 37·9 ___ 38

i 44·2 ___ 44·3

j 56 ___ 56·1

2 Order these groups of decimal fractions from smallest to largest.

a	b	c	d	e
6·85	19·04	35·09	46·13	67·92
6·58	19·08	35·99	64·33	68·98
6·88	20·01	35·19	46·31	60·90
6·55	19·28	35·29	44·30	86·94
6·80	20·48	35·89	46·03	76·93
6·50	20·14	35·90	64·23	80·09

Refresher

1 Copy out the number lines filling in the missing numbers. The first one is done for you.

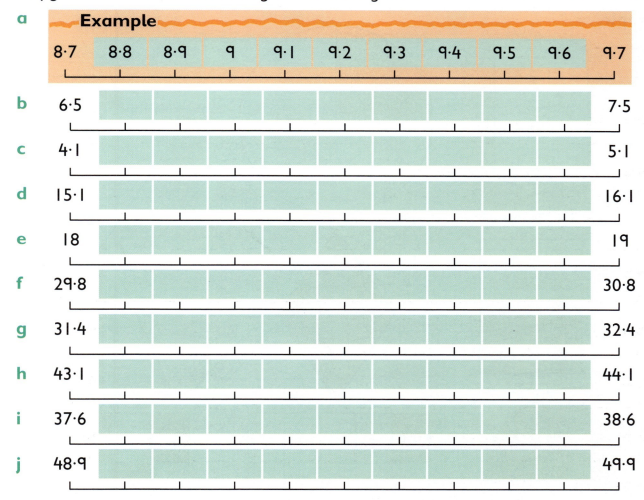

a Example
8·7 | 8·8 | 8·9 | 9 | 9·1 | 9·2 | 9·3 | 9·4 | 9·5 | 9·6 | 9·7

b 6·5 ... 7·5

c 4·1 ... 5·1

d 15·1 ... 16·1

e 18 ... 19

f 29·8 ... 30·8

g 31·4 ... 32·4

h 43·1 ... 44·1

i 37·6 ... 38·6

j 48·9 ... 49·9

2 Order these groups of decimal fractions from smallest to largest.

a	b	c	d	e
6·3	6·7	13·8	81·7	25·6
7·3	9·1	13·1	18·1	24·7
3·6	9·5	14	81·2	25·8
5·6	5·1	14·3	18·5	23·9
7·6	5·9	13·6	18·7	25·2

Challenge

1 Write the decimal fractions in exercise 2 of the Practice section as fractions.

Example

$6·85 = 6\frac{85}{100}$

Percentages

Practice

Remember

100% is the whole shape

What per cent of each shape has been shaded? What per cent has not been shaded?

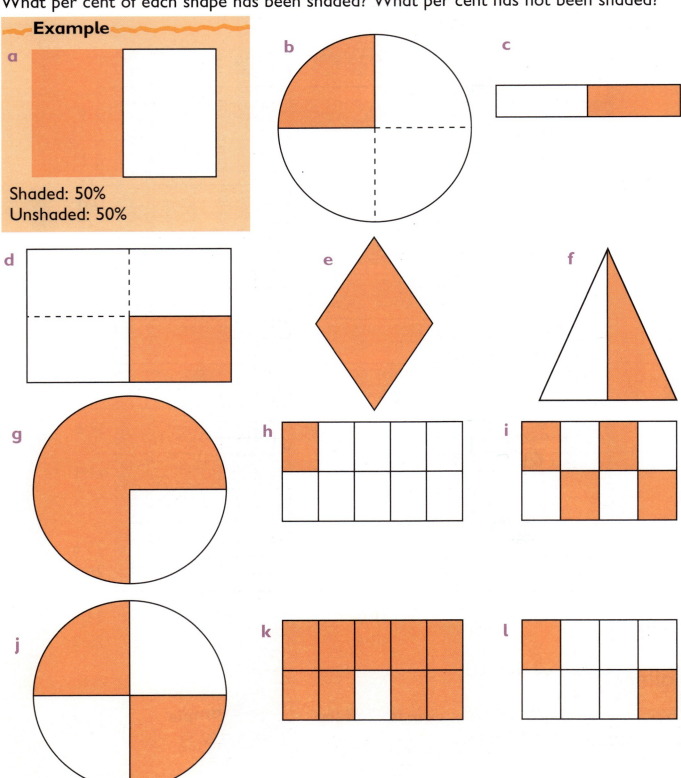

Example

a

Shaded: 50%
Unshaded: 50%

Refresher

What per cent of each grid has been shaded?
What per cent has not been shaded?

a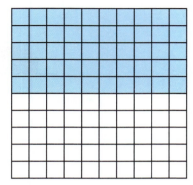

b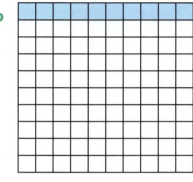

c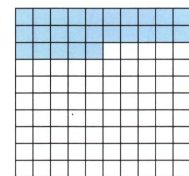

d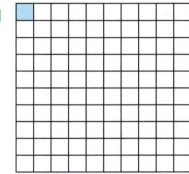

e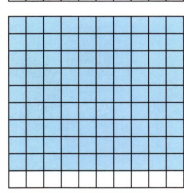

f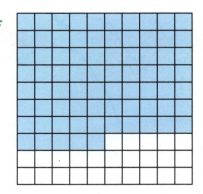

Challenge

Write the percentages as fractions
and decimal fractions.

Example

$10\% = \frac{10}{100} = 0\cdot1$

50%   25%   20%   75%   90%   30%   80%   40%   60%   70%

Shop percentages

Practice

1 Work out 50% of these prices.

a £12
b £26
c £9
d £21
e £30
f £64
g £15
h £92
i £108
j £120

2 Work out 25% of these prices.

a RADIO £20
b STEREO CASSETTE £12
c PERSONAL STEREO £10
d FM/MW/LW TUNER £24
e CLOCK/RADIO £40
f RADIO/CASSETTE £32
g 10 PACK MINIDISCS £16
h VIDEO PACK £22
i CORDLESS PHONE £18
j £100

STAR BUY! Long Play Video ONLY

Refresher

Find 50% of these amounts.

Remember

50% is half.

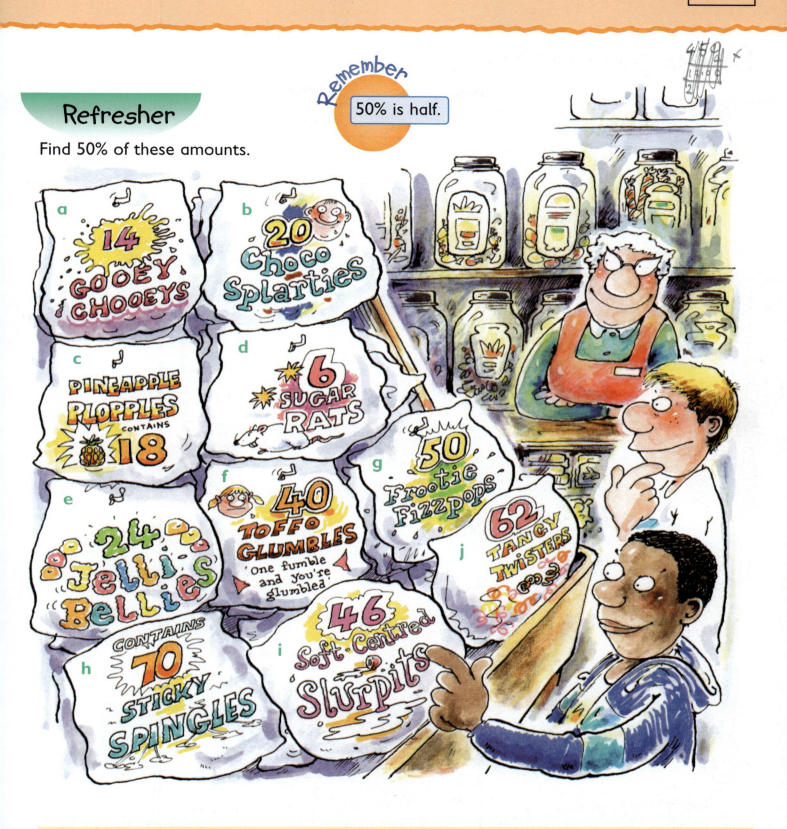

a **14 GOOEY CHOOEYS**

b **20 Choco Splarties**

c **PINEAPPLE PLOPPLES CONTAINS 18**

d **6 SUGAR RATS**

e **24 Jelli Bellies**

f **40 TOFFO GLUMBLES** One fumble and you're glumbled

g **50 Frootie Fizzpops**

h **CONTAINS 70 STICKY SPINGLES**

i **46 Soft-Centred Slurpits**

j **62 TANGY TWISTERS**

Challenge

Find 10% of all the prices in the Practice section.

Example
10% of £12 = £1·20 (£1·20 × 10 = £12)

43

Race to 100%

Practice

You need:
- a 10 × 10 grid each
- I die marked 25%, 25%, 10%, 10%, 10%, 5%
- a coloured pencil each

What to do

Play the game in twos or threes.
- Take it in turns to throw the die and colour in that per cent of your grid.
- The winner is the first player to colour all of their grid. Remember you must be able to colour 100% exactly with your last throw!

Refresher

What percentage of the shapes on the children's jumpers are red?

Challenge

Play the game **Race to 100%** in the Practice section on a 2 × 10 grid.

Work out these before you play.

a What is 25% of the grid?

b What is 10% of the grid?

c What is 5% of the grid?

In proportion

Practice

1 Cereal bars come in packs of 8. Out of every packet, I eat 7 cereal bars and my mum eats 1. Copy and complete the table.

   a How many cereal bars have I eaten if my mum has eaten 8?

   b How many cereal bars has my mum eaten if I have eaten 70?

Me	Mum
7	1
14	

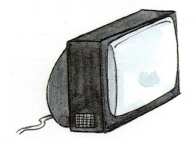

2 For every 5 minutes I spend tidying my room, I can watch 10 minutes of television. Copy and complete the table.

   a Tonight I can watch 100 minutes of television. How much time did I spend tidying my room?

   b If I spend 40 minutes tidying my room, for how long will I be able to watch television?

Tidying room	T.V.
5	10
10	

3 Every time I buy 2 goldfish for my pond, I buy 4 new plants. Copy and complete the table showing the proportion of fish to plants in my pond.

   a When I have 48 plants how many fish will there be?

   b If I get 20 fish how many plants will I need?

Fish	Plants
2	4

Refresher

1 For every 1p Philip saves, his brother Tim saves 5p.
Copy and complete the table showing their savings.

Philip	Tim
1p	5p

2 For every 1 chocolate bar Chris eats, Karen eats 3.
Copy and complete the table.

Chris	Karen
1	3

3 When we go swimming, for every 1 length I swim,
my friend swims 4. Copy and complete the table.

Me	My friend
1	4

Challenge

54 tiles can fit on my kitchen floor. I want to put
3 blue tiles for every 6 white tiles.

How many of each colour tile will I need to buy?

Use a 6 × 9 piece of squared paper to plan my
kitchen floor.

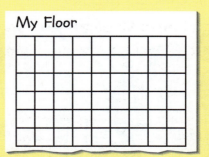

My Floor

Use the proportion

Practice

Work out the problems using the proportions given.

1 There are 30 children going on the school outing. For every 2 boys going there are 4 girls. How many boys and how many girls are going?

2 In every bag of apples you buy, there are 2 red apples and 5 green. I buy 4 bags. How many of each colour will I have?

3 In the staffroom, for every one cup of tea drunk, seven cups of coffee are drunk. Today 5 cups of tea have been drunk. How many cups of coffee have been drunk?

4 A box of chocolates has 3 toffee-filled chocolates for every 5 nut-filled ones. I buy a box of 24 chocolates. How many of each chocolate will I have?

5 At Park Vale school, for every 6 children, 4 wear uniform and 2 do not. In one class of 30 how many children will be wearing uniform and how many will not?

Refresher

Work out the problems. You may want to copy and complete the table to help you.

1 Rachel is mixing pink paint. For every spoonful of red paint she puts in 4 spoonfuls of white.
If she puts in 7 spoons of red how many white will she put in?

Red	White
1	4
2	
3	
4	
5	
6	
7	

2 Tim is feeding his cat and her kitten cat sweets. For every 1 sweet he gives the kitten, he gives the cat 3. He has 24 sweets to share. How many will they each have?

Cat	Kitten
3	1

3 Dad has made 6 cakes. On every cake he puts 1 cherry and 2 choc chips. How many of each will he need?

Cherries	Choc chips
1	2

Challenge

I am making a table cloth by sewing squares together. For every 3 orange squares I have 2 red. Altogether I have 50 squares.

a Design my table cloth.

b What fraction of the tablecloth is red?

c What fraction of the tablecloth is orange?

d What percentage of the tablecloth is red?

e What percentage of the tablecloth is orange?

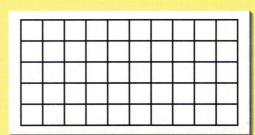

Chance

Practice

1 Which of these words mean the same as the ones in the box?

- **a** unlikely
- **b** impossible
- **c** certain
- **d** likely

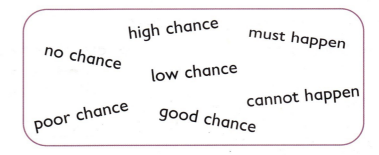

high chance   must happen

no chance   low chance

poor chance   good chance   cannot happen

2 Copy the scale and then write the letters on it.

no chance	poor chance	good chance	certain

A

You will come to school at midnight.

B

You will be late for school one day.

C

You will leave school today.

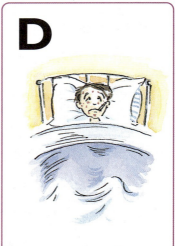

D

You will be off sick all next week.

3 How likely are these to happen?

- **a** You will be a millionaire.
- **b** You will be given some money next year.
- **c** You will write a cheque for over £500.
- **d** You will own all the money in the world.

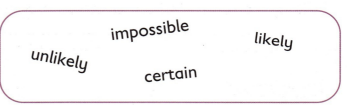

impossible   likely

unlikely   certain

4 What are the chances of these happening?

- **a** You will learn to drive.
- **b** You can pass your driving test blindfold.
- **c** You will see a car next week.
- **d** You will learn to fly.

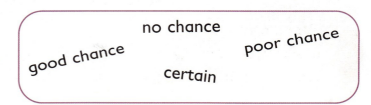

no chance   poor chance

good chance   certain

Refresher

1 Which of these are impossible?

a break a leg

b grow two heads

c grow taller

2 Which of these are certain?

a meet Queen Victoria

b meet the Prime Minister

c see someone tomorrow

3 Which of these are unlikely?

a moon will crash into the Earth

b you will see a meteor next year

c the moon will shine tonight

4 Which of these are likely?

a you will get older

b you will live longer than your teacher

c you will get younger

5 Copy the scale. Write the letters in question 4 on it.

no chance	poor chance	good chance	certain

Challenge

1 Copy the table. Write three descriptions in each column.

No chance	Poor chance	Good chance	Certain

Football bar charts

Practice

Work in pairs.

You need:
● Resource Copymaster 7
● a die each with the numbers 0, 0, 1, 1, 2, 2

1 Each of you roll the die to give the results of a football match, for example 2–1. Add the goals up. Do this 40 times.

2 + 1 = 3
We scored a total of 3 goals.

2 Record the total goals scored in this tally chart.

Total goals scored	Tally	Frequency
0		
1		
2		
3		

3 Copy and complete this bar chart.

4 **a** How many times was the total number of goals scored 2?

b In how many matches were no goals scored?

c What is the mode?

d In how many matches were less than 2 goals scored?

e In how many matches were 1 or more goals scored?

f Which total number of goals has the lowest frequency?

Total goals scored

Number of matches (vertical axis: 0, 2, 4, 6, 8, 10, 12, 14, 16, 18, 20)

Total number of goals (horizontal axis: 0, 1, 2, 3, 4)

Refresher

Work in pairs.

You need:
- Resource Copymaster 7
- a die each numbered 0, 0, 1, 1, 2, 3

1 Each of you roll the die to give the results of a football match, for example 0–1. Do this 20 times.

2 Draw this chart in your book. Record the goals each team scores.

Goals scored	Tally	Frequency
0		
1		
2		
3		

3 Copy and complete this bar chart.

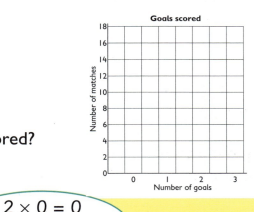

Goals scored

4 **a** How many teams scored 3 goals?

   b How many teams did not score a goal?

   c How many teams scored 1 or 2 goals?

   d What is the most common number of goals scored?

   e What is your answer to d called?

Challenge

Work in pairs.

You need:
- Resource copymaster 7
- a die each numbered 0, 0, 1, 1, 2, 3

$2 \times 0 = 0$
The product is 0.

1 Each of you roll the die. Calculate the product of the numbers. Do this 30 times.

2 Record the products in a tally chart.

3 Draw a bar chart to show your results.

4 **a** How many times was the product 4?

   b How many times was the product below 3?

   c What is the least common product?

   d What is the **mode**?

   e How many times was the product 5? Explain your answer.

Bird bar line charts

Practice

1 The bar line chart shows the worms collected by blackbirds.
Copy and complete the table.

Worms	Number of times collected
1	
2	
3	
4	
5	
6	

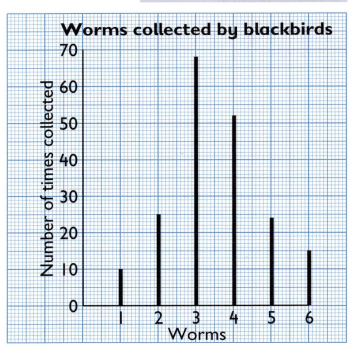

Worms collected by blackbirds

2 The table shows the worms collected by sparrows. Copy and complete the bar line chart onto Resource Copymaster 8.

Worms	Number of times collected
1	15
2	70
3	49
4	22
5	5

3 a How many blackbirds collected 3 worms?

b Did more or less sparrows collect 3 worms?

c What is the most common number of worms collected by blackbirds?

d What is the mode for sparrows?

e How many blackbirds collected less than 4 worms?

f How many times did sparrows visit the garden altogether?

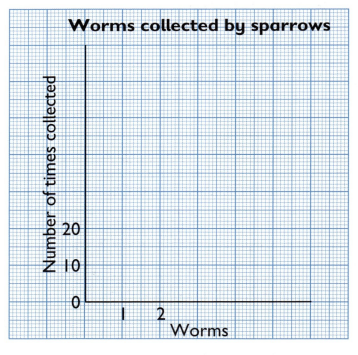

Worms collected by sparrows

Refresher

1 The bar line chart shows the birds Dianne spotted. Copy and complete the table.

Bird	Number
thrush	
blackbird	
sparrow	
starling	
robin	

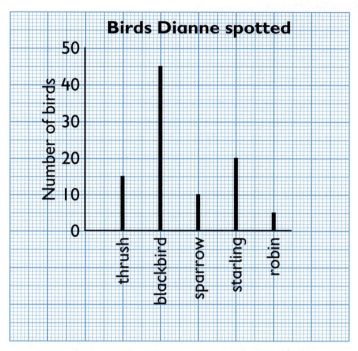

Birds Dianne spotted

2 The table shows the birds Atul spotted. Copy and complete the bar line chart onto Resource Copymaster 8.

Bird	Number
thrush	40
blackbird	75
sparrow	20
starling	35
robin	15

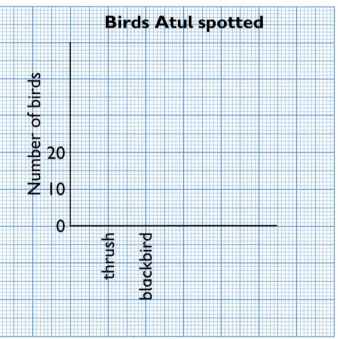

Birds Atul spotted

3 a How many starlings did Dianne spot?
  b How many robins did Atul spot?
  c Which bird did Dianne spot most?
  d Which bird did Atul spot 35 times?
  e Atul spotted more thrushes than Dianne. How many more?
  f How many birds did Dianne spot altogether?

Challenge

1 Combine Dianne and Atul's results. Draw a bar line chart. Number the vertical axis in steps of 20.

Personal databases

Practice

These tables show children's test scores.

Mental test scores			
Anila	9	Iris	6
Chris	8	Gary	8
Kate	6	Fay	6
Jim	5	Darren	10
Hattie	2	Bela	5

Spelling test scores			
Gary	7	Jim	8
Hattie	10	Iris	3
Bela	7	Darren	4
Fay	6	Kate	7
Chris	10	Anila	8

1 Copy and complete this database.

Name	Mental test score	Spelling test score
Anila	9	8
Bela		

2 a Which children scored 8 in the spelling test?

   b How many children scored above 6 in the mental test?

   c What is the mode for the mental test scores?

   d What is the mode for the spelling test scores?

   e What is the lowest mental test score?

   f What is the highest spelling test score?

   g Which children did better in the spelling test than in the mental test?

   h Which children scored a total of 12 in both tests?

   i Who got the highest total score?

Refresher

This database contains information about Maria's friends.

Name	Way of travelling to school	Time to travel to school (minutes)	Distances travelled to school (km)
Cindy	bus	20	2
Eddie	bus	15	$1\frac{1}{2}$
Jane	cycle	10	1
Leroy	car	15	2
Mike	walk	5	$\frac{1}{2}$
Paula	walk	10	$\frac{1}{2}$
Shuky	bus	15	2

1 Copy the database.

2 Add your own name. Write how you travel to school, how long it takes and how far you travel.

3 a What is the longest travel time?

   b Who lives $\frac{1}{2}$ km from school?

   c How does Leroy travel to school?

   d What is the most common way of travelling to school?

   e What is the most common distance travelled? What is this number called?

   f What is the mode for the time taken?

   g How many children travel for longer than 10 minutes?

Challenge

Make a database about famous people from history.

1 Choose ten famous people from an encyclopedia.

2 Find out their dates of birth and death. Add them to the database.

3 Work out their ages. Add them to the database.

   a Who lived the longest?

   b Who lived the shortest?

   c Who was born first?

Name	Born	Died	Age
Beethoven	1770	1827	57

   d Who died last?

   e How many people lived longer than 60 years?

Game results databases

Practice

Work in groups.

You need:
● a timer

1 Choose a partner and play this game.
   Set the timer for 5 minutes. Play as many games as you can.

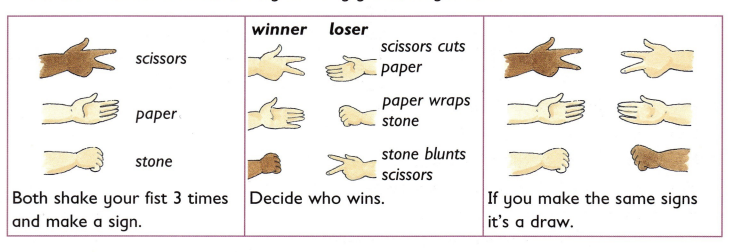

2 Record your own results like this. W L L D W W
   Use W for Win, L for Lose, D for Draw.

3 Count your wins, losses and draws.

4 Make a database for the group. Each
   person fills in their results, like this:

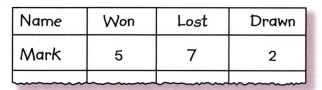

Name	Won	Lost	Drawn
Mark	5	7	2

5 a Who won the most games?

   b Who drew the least number of games?

   c How many children lost more than 5 games?

   d What is the mode for the number of games won?

   e What is the mode for the number of games lost?

   f What is the mode for the number of games drawn?

   g How many games were lost altogether?

   h Who drew more times than they won?

   i How many games were played altogether?

I win!

Refresher

This database shows the results of some games of draughts.

Name	Won	Lost	Drawn
April	3	0	0
Charles	3	1	1
Hoda	4	0	0
Jill	0	5	3
Oliver	1	3	1
Raj	0	2	1
Sam	2	2	0
Tess	2	3	2
Val	1	2	3
Zoë	3	1	1

1 How many games did Jill lose?

2 How many games did Val win?

3 How many games did Charles draw?

4 How many games did Hoda play altogether?

5 Which children won the most games?

6 What is the mode for the number of lost games?

7 What is the mode for the number of drawn games?

8 How many games were won altogether?

9 Who won and lost the same number of games?

Challenge

Work in groups.

1 For ten minutes, play the same game as in Practice.

2 Record your own results like this.
   W(Sc) means you won using scissors.

3 Make a database for the group.

Name	Won	Lost	Drawn	Scissors	Paper	Stone
Mark	5	7	2	6	5	3

4 Calculate the modes for each column.

Calculator challenge

Practice

1 Copy the number grid and play this game.

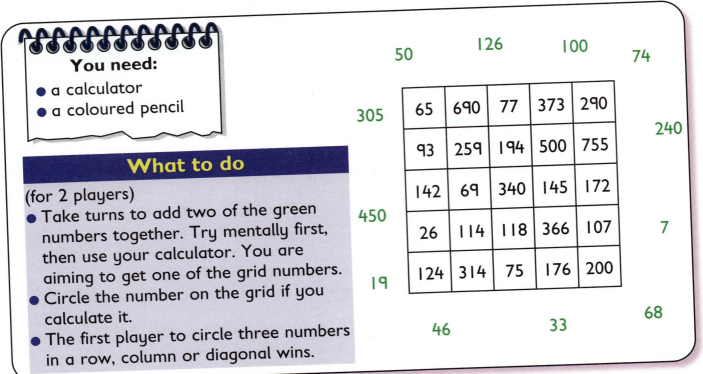

You need:
- a calculator
- a coloured pencil

What to do

(for 2 players)
- Take turns to add two of the green numbers together. Try mentally first, then use your calculator. You are aiming to get one of the grid numbers.
- Circle the number on the grid if you calculate it.
- The first player to circle three numbers in a row, column or diagonal wins.

Green numbers: 50 126 100 74 305 240 450 19 7 46 33 68

65	690	77	373	290
93	259	194	500	755
142	69	340	145	172
26	114	118	366	107
124	314	75	176	200

2 Play the game using this grid. Subtract these numbers.

Green numbers: 300 16 101 8 92 20 135 47

84	119	81	253
208	45	199	43
31	88	93	4
9	27	115	76

3 Multiply these numbers.

Green numbers: 5 19 36 7 11 100 31 10

3100	209	217	55
1116	77	190	700
180	396	1000	133
35	155	589	110

4 Go back to each grid. Use your calculator to add up the grid numbers you circled. Who got the largest total?

Refresher

You need:
- a calculator

1 Copy the grid.

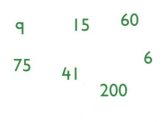

9   15   60

75   41   6

200

a Add pairs of the green numbers together.
Try mentally first. Use your calculator if you need to.

b Write your answers in the grid.

c Circle the answer if you calculated it mentally.

2 Draw another grid.
This time, multiply pairs of numbers together.

Challenge

(for 2 players)

1 Copy the number grid and play this game.

29   51   146   92

40   235   17

95	97	143	75
381	206	89	80
46	275	106	121
11	63	286	195

You need:
- a calculator
- a coloured pencil

a Take turns to add or subtract two of the green numbers. Try mentally first. Then use your calculator. You are aiming to get one of the grid numbers.

b Circle a grid number you calculate.

c The first person to circle three numbers in a row, column or diagonal wins.

2 Go back and take turns to calculate the missing grid numbers.
Circle each one with your colour.

3 Use your calculator to add up the grid numbers you circled. Who got the largest total?

Calculating costs

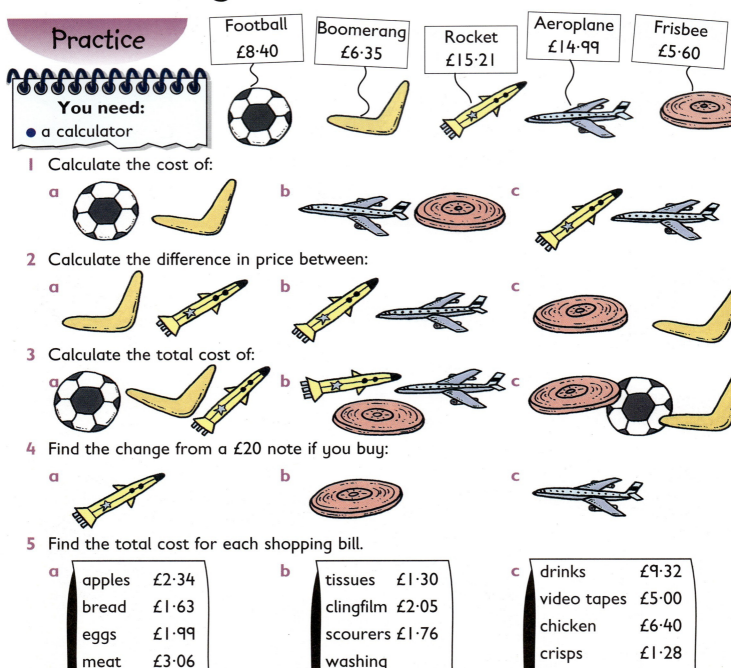

Practice

You need:
● a calculator

Football £8·40
Boomerang £6·35
Rocket £15·21
Aeroplane £14·99
Frisbee £5·60

1 Calculate the cost of:

a   b   c

2 Calculate the difference in price between:

a   b   c

3 Calculate the total cost of:

a   b   c

4 Find the change from a £20 note if you buy:

a   b   c

5 Find the total cost for each shopping bill.

a
apples	£2·34
bread	£1·63
eggs	£1·99
meat	£3·06
Total	_____

b
tissues	£1·30
clingfilm	£2·05
scourers	£1·76
washing powder	£3·99
Total	_____

c
drinks	£9·32
video tapes	£5·00
chicken	£6·40
crisps	£1·28
nuts	£3·00
Total	_____

6 The total cost is shown. Calculate the cost of one object.

a  £2·76   b  £9·92   c  £7

Refresher

Use your calculator to work out these.

1 a £1·32 + £2·51   b £9·63 + £4·11   c £3·85 + £5·19   d £1·97 + £4·80

2 a £6·59 + £2·75   b £19·99 − £8·52   c £3·01 − £1·03   d £24·62 − £16·50

3 a 3 × £1·24   b 5 × £3·99   c 2 × £51·73   d 7 × £2·01

4 a £6·25 ÷ 5   b £12·34 ÷ 2   c £5·44 ÷ 4   d £42·67 ÷ 17

Challenge

You need:
● a calculator

£4·16

£1·28

£2·60

£1·83

£8·99

£11·41

£1·75

1 You have a £5 note to spend.
   Buy some things and work out the change.

2 Buy more things with another £5 note. Spend as much as you can. Work out the change.

3 Repeat question 2. What things can you buy that will give you the least change from your £5?

4 Start with a £10 note. Repeat question 2.

5 Start with a £20 note. Repeat question 2.

Money calculations

Practice

You need:
● a calculator

1 Calculate the answers in pence. Change pounds to pence first.

   a 72p + £1·84   b 60p + £4·48   c £2·20 + 151p
   d £2·25 + 95p   e £5·63 + 117p   f 8p + £8·96

2 Convert your answers to question 1 to pounds and pence.

3 Calculate these answers in pounds and pence. Change pence to pounds first.

   a £3·44 + 172p   b £2·50 + 465p   c £1·56 + 71p
   d 49p + £6·98   e 87p + £3·23   f 40p + £12·70

4 Give your answers in pounds and pence.

   a £1·34 + 263p + 159p   b 152p + £7·10 + £2·28   c 75p + £1·20 + 86p
   d £4·99 + £1·50 + 66p   e £1·25 + 29p + £3·21 + 48p   f 6p + £4·16 + £1·21 + £7

5 Calculate the difference in price.

   a   b   c   d

£3·34   198p

76p   £2·51

95p   £2·25

£3   84p

6 Nancy saves 85p every week. How much does she save in:

   a 5 weeks   b 12 weeks   c 40 weeks

   Give your answers in pounds and pence.

7 These children saved the same amount every week.
   How much did they save each week?

   a   b   c   d

£7·85

5 weeks

£8·40

10 weeks

£20·90

22 weeks

£60

50 weeks

Refresher

Use your calculator to work out these.

1 Change these amounts to pence.

a £2·41   b £9·23   c £4·20   d £1·90
e £0·23   f £0·99   g £5   h £10

2 Change these amounts to pounds and pence.

a 516p   b 293p   c 610p   d 350p
e 62p   f 15p   g 70p   h 200p

3 Calculate these.
Change your answers to pounds and pence.

a 90p + 47p   b 265p − 99p   c 348p ÷ 4   d 9 × 57p
e 150p + 70p   f 320p − 245p   g 410 ÷ 5   h 6 × 15p

Challenge

You will need a calculator. Calculate the total shopping bill.

a
Milk	£1·75
Cheese	£2·36
Spinach	94p
Meat	£5·20
Cereal	£2·07
Cola	£0·35
Plug	60p
Total	

b
Eggs	58p
Cream	£1·42
Fruit	430p
Wine	£8
Matches	80p
Vegetables	£6·30
Total	

c
Ham	300p
Clothes	£16·20
Garlic	30p
Frozen meals	£10·05
Chocolate	70p
Carrier bag	9p
Cake	£3·96
Total	

All about rectangles

Practice

The end branches of this decision tree show the sorting of some triangles and quadrilaterals.

1 Use the decision tree to name these shapes.

a It has parallel sides. It has right angles. It is blue.

b It has no parallel sides. All sides are equal. It is not blue.

c It has parallel sides, right angles and all sides are equal.

d It has no parallel sides. It has a right angle. It is blue.

2 Write a description for these shapes.

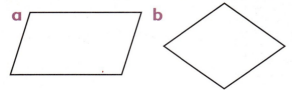

a   b

3 On which branch will these shapes finish?

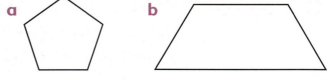

a   b

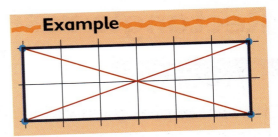

Example

Refresher

1 Draw these diagonals on 1 cm squared paper.

2 Use a ruler to draw the four sides of the quadrilateral.

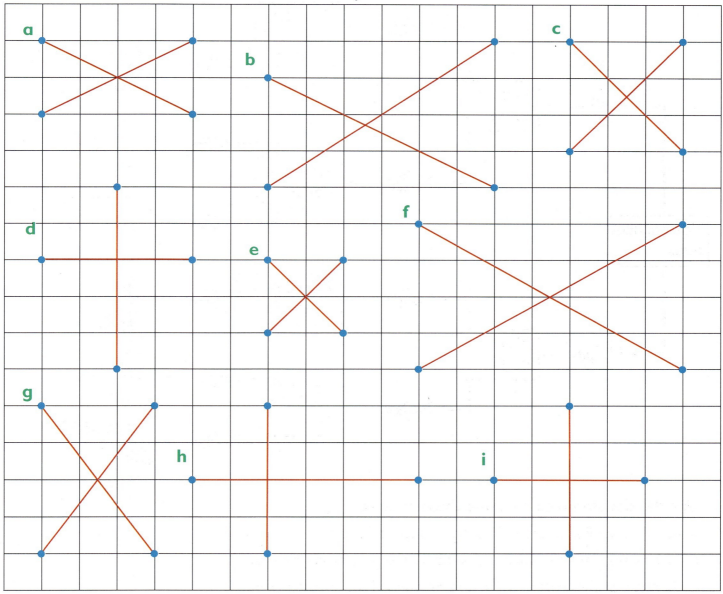

3 Write the letter of the quadrilaterals which are:

   a rectangles   b squares

Challenge

Only in quadrilaterals which are rectangles will the second diagonal bisect the first diagonal into two equal parts.

True or false? Investigate

Rectangle research

You need:
- a supply of squares or cubes
- I cm squared paper

Practice

1 *With 12 squares you can make 3 different rectangles.*

True or false?

Draw each different rectangle on squared paper.
Record your results in a table.

2 a *24 squares can be arranged to make exactly 4 different rectangles.*

Investigate.
Draw each different rectangle on squared paper. Make a table of your results.

length in squares	width in squares
6	4

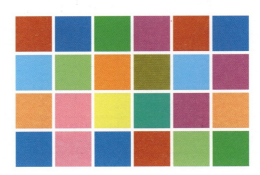

b **What if ... you had 36 squares?**

How many different rectangles can you make?
Draw the rectangles and make a table.

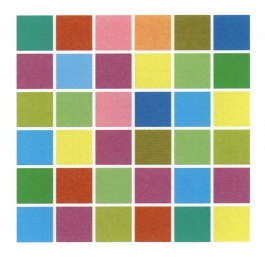

c **What if ... you had 48 squares?**

Can you make exactly 6 different rectangles?
Do not draw the rectangles.
List their dimensions in a table.

3 Count all the squares in this diagram
Work in a systematic way.
Begin with the smallest size of square.

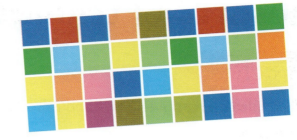

Refresher

You need:
- 36 squares

1 Arrange the squares to make a rectangle.

2 Count how many squares make up the length and how many squares make up the width.

3 Record your results in a table.

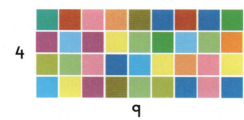

width in squares	length in squares
4	9

4 a Use the same 36 squares to make different rectangles. Find as many as you can.

   b Keep a record in the table.

Challenge

1 Count all the rectangles in this diagram. Work in a systematic way. Begin with the smallest rectangle. Use the diagrams below to help you.

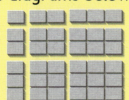

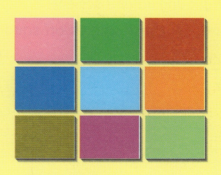

2 Copy and complete this table for the rectangles you find.

	length in units		
width in units	1	2	3
1			
2			
3			
total			

3 Write about the patterns you notice.

All sorts of triangles

Practice

1 *A triangle can be right-angled and isosceles.*

Copy these right angles on to squared paper.

Draw one more line to make a right-angled triangle.

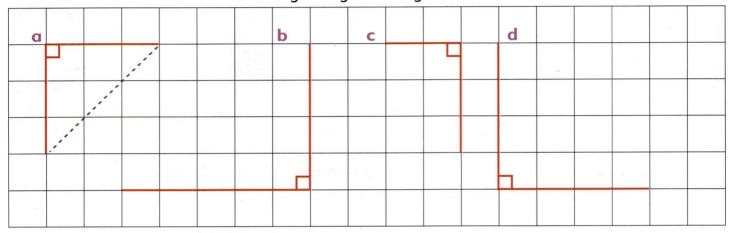

Now check if the generalisation is true or false.

2 *A triangle can be right-angled and scalene.*

In the same way, draw these angles on squared paper and complete the triangle.

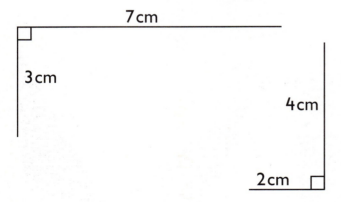

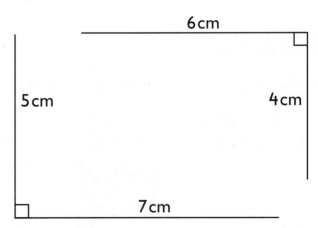

Is the statement true or false?

3 Look at these Venn diagrams.

Decide which is correct. Give a reason for your answer.

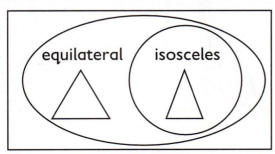

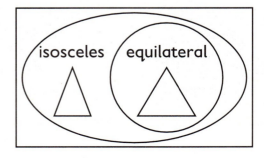

Refresher

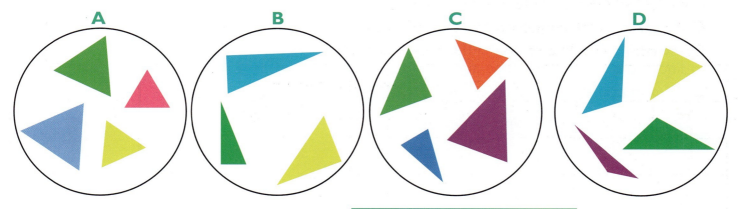

1 Look at the sets of triangles. Copy and
complete this table for sets A to D.

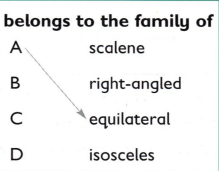

belongs to the family of

A   scalene

B   right-angled

C   equilateral

D   isosceles

Challenge

Write the family to which each of these shapes belongs.

Example

a – isosceles

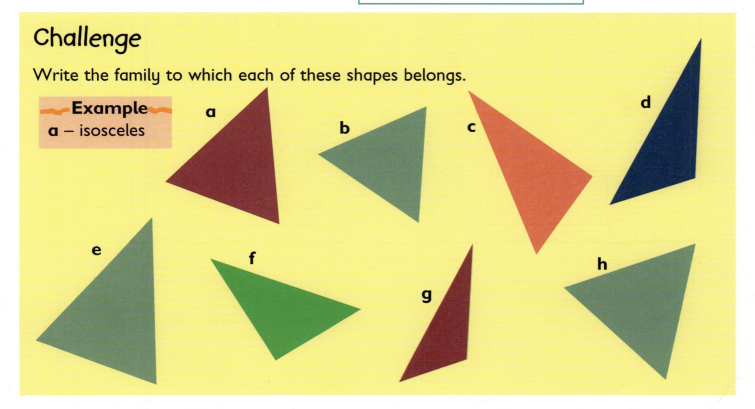

Symmetry in triangles

Practice

1 Copy this square on to dot square paper. Draw straight lines to make 3 triangles. Cut out the triangles. Check by folding to find if the triangle has line symmetry. Copy and complete this table.

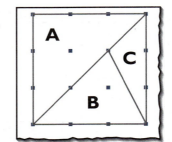

You need:
- I cm dot square paper

Triangle	Type	has line symmetry
A	isosceles	yes
B		
C		

2 Copy, cut out, fold and record these squares and rectangles in the same way.

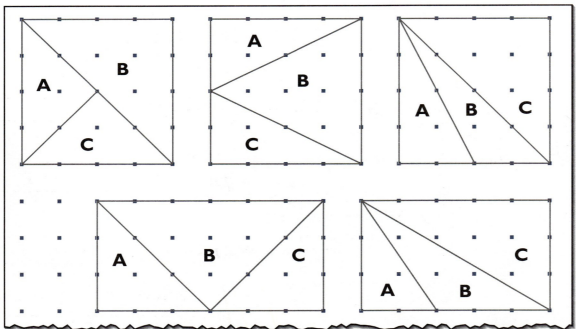

Refresher

I Use the Decision tree to sort these six triangles.
Write the name of the triangle for each end branch.
The first one is done for you.

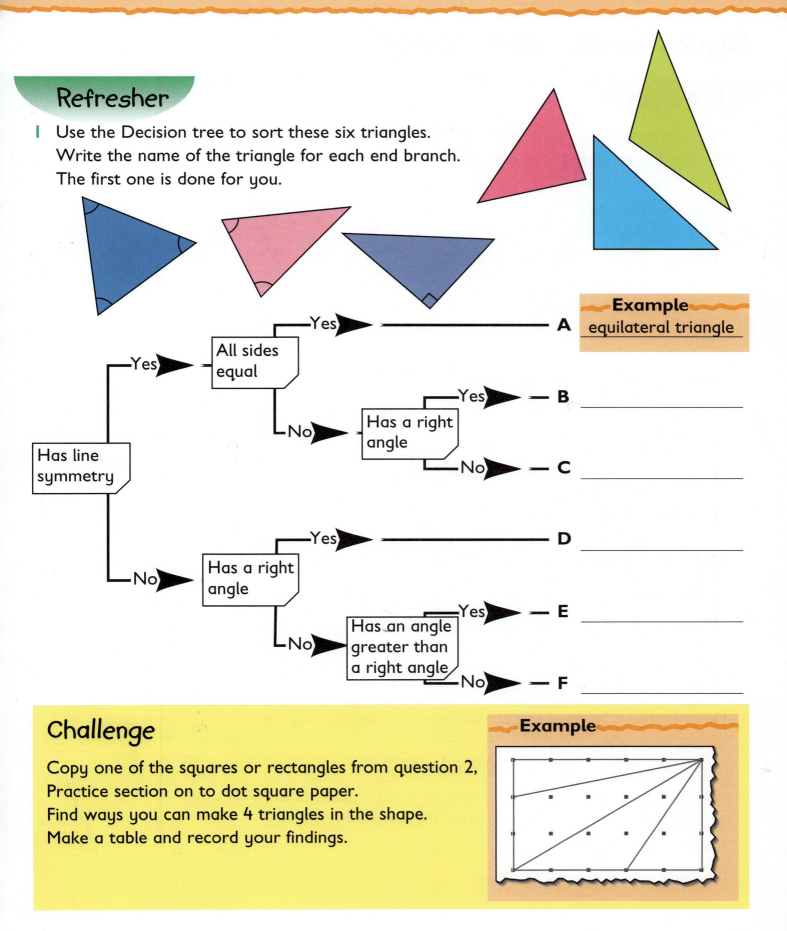

Example
equilateral triangle

A _____

B _____

C _____

D _____

E _____

F _____

Challenge

Copy one of the squares or rectangles from question 2,
Practice section on to dot square paper.
Find ways you can make 4 triangles in the shape.
Make a table and record your findings.

Example

73

Cantilever patterns

Practice

You need:
● a supply of matchsticks
● a sheet of dot paper

Work with a partner.

1 Make these three patterns with your sticks.

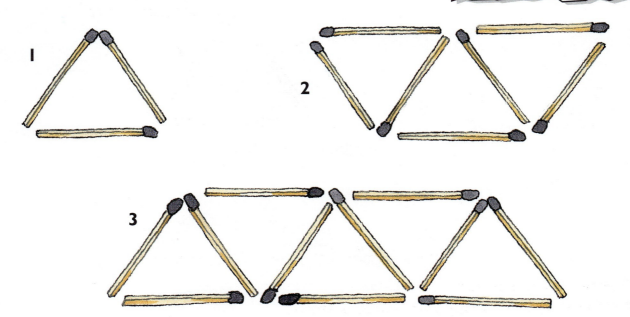

2 Make the next two cantilever bridge patterns in the sequence with your sticks.

3 Draw your 5 patterns on to dot paper.

4 Copy and complete the table for the first 5 triangles.

pattern number	1	2	3	4	5	.... 10 ....
number of sticks	3	7				

difference   4

4 Describe the difference pattern to your partner and together decide on a rule.

Write down your rule and check it.

5 Use your rule to predict the number of sticks needed to build a cantilever bridge: of pattern number 10, pattern number 25.

Check your answers.

Refresher

You need:
- a supply of matchsticks
- a sheet of dot paper

Work with a partner.

1 Make these three patterns with your sticks.

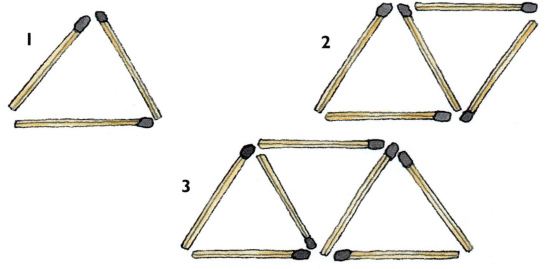

2 Decide how the pattern is built up.
Build the next two cantilever bridge patterns
in the sequence with your sticks.

3 Copy all five patterns on to dot paper.

4 Copy and complete this table.

number of triangles	number of sticks
1	3
2	
3	
4	
5	

5 Predict the number of sticks you will need
to build a cantilever bridge with 6 triangles.

Challenge

Suppose you had 79 sticks. You use them all to build a cantilever bridge.
How many triangles will there be? Explain, in writing, how you worked it out.

Plotting the points

Practice

1 a Copy the first grid on to Resource Copymaster 11.
Write down the co-ordinates of each point.

> **Example**
> C (2, 4)

b Plot these points on the same grid.
(3, 0), (3, 1), (3, 2), (3, 3), (3, 4), (3, 5)
Draw a straight line through the points.
Name the axis to which the line is parallel.

c On the same grid, mark the points (0, 0) and (6, 6).
Join them with a straight line. Write the co-ordinates of the points
where the diagonal line crosses the other two lines.

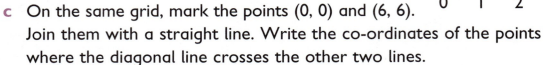

2 Some multiples of ×6 table are
plotted on this grid.

> **Example**
> $6 \times 2 = 12$ is the point (1, 2)
> $6 \times 3 = 18$ is the point (1, 8)

a Copy the grid on to Resource
Copymaster 12.

b Continue it as far as you can.

c Write the co-ordinates of the
points where the pattern
repeats.

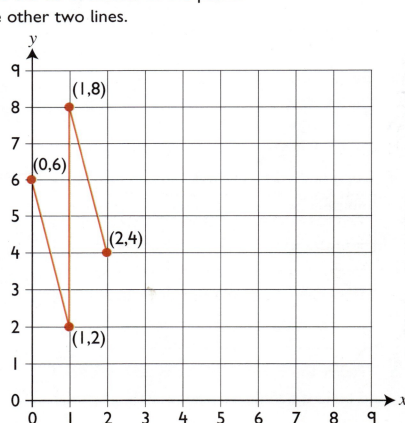

3 a Copy and continue this table to 8×10.

b Label each axis as in question 2.

c Plot the points on a new grid on Resource Copymaster 12.

d Write about patterns you notice.

$8 \times 1 = 8$ (0, 8)

$8 \times 2 = 16$ (1, 6)

$8 \times 3 = 24$ (2, 4)

... and so on.

Refresher

These are the positions of some yachts during a race.

1 Write down the co-ordinates of yachts A, B, C and D.

Example
yacht A (2, 5)

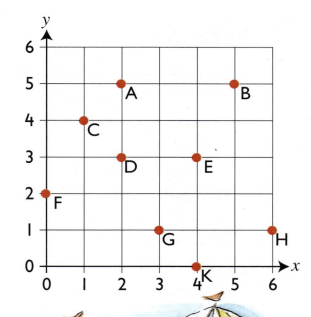

2 Copy and complete.

a Yachts with x-co-ordinate 2

D (2, ⬜) and ⬜ (2, ⬜).

b Yachts with y-co-ordinate 1

⬜ (⬜ , 1) and ⬜ (⬜ , 1).

c Yacht with x-co-ordinate zero

⬜ (⬜ , ⬜)

d Yacht with y-co-ordinate zero

⬜ (⬜ , ⬜)

d Yacht with same x and y co-ordinates

⬜ (⬜ , ⬜)

Challenge

a On Resource Copymaster 12 plot these points. (3, 0), (9, 6) and (3, 6)

b Join the points with a straight line.

c Write down the co-ordinates of all the points each line passes through.

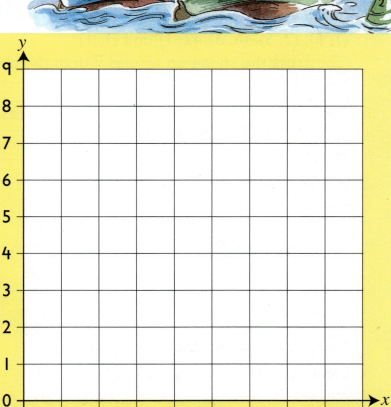

Shapely plotting

Practice

1 Copy this grid on to Resource Copymaster 12.

   a Construct square A drawing sides parallel to the axes.

   b List the co-ordinates of the vertices in a clockwise order.

2 Construct 3 more squares B, C and D in the grid making each square a different size and colour.

3 Three of the vertices of a square are (2, 1), (2, 4) and (5, 4). Construct the square. Write the co-ordinates of the 4th vertex.

4 a These points are the co-ordinates of the vertices of a shape.
   (1, 5), (2, 5), (4, 3), (2, 1) and (1, 1)
   Construct the shape on to grid 7. Join the points in a clockwise order.
   Name the shape you have drawn.

   b Repeat, as above, for this set of co-ordinates.
   (1, 3), (5, 7), (7, 5) and (3, 1).

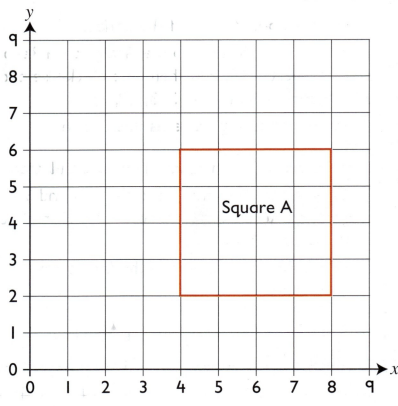

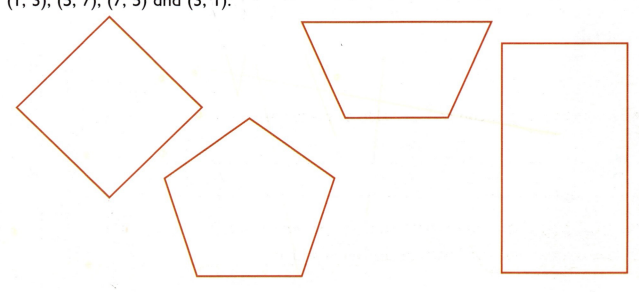

Refresher

1 **a** List the co-ordinates of this shape.

b Plot these points on to the first grid on Resource Copymaster 11. Join them in a clockwise order to make a shape. (1, 1) (1, 3), (3, 3), (3, 1).

c Write about any patterns you notice.

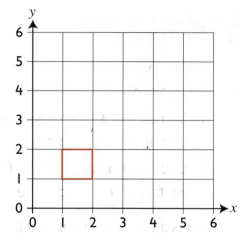

2 3 of the vertices of a square have been plotted.

a Copy these diagrams on to the 2nd and 3rd grids on Resource Copymaster 11. Complete the square in each case.

b Write the co-ordinates of the 4th vertex of each square.

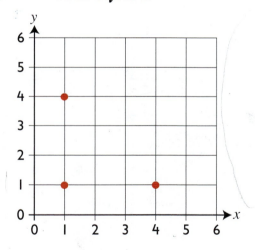
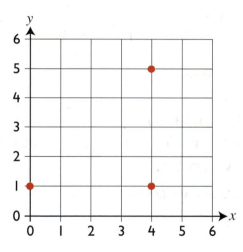

Challenge

In these diagrams you can see one side of a square.

A (4, 5)   B (9, 5)   A (3, 7)   B (9, 7)

Write your first choice of co-ordinates for points C and D.

Now find a different set of vertices for each shape.

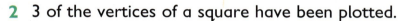

Rectangle round-up

Practice

1 Copy and complete these rectangles on 1 cm squared paper.
The perimeters are given for each rectangle.

a
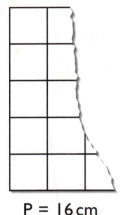
P = 16 cm

b
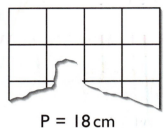
P = 18 cm

c
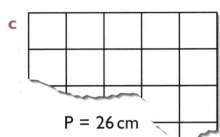
P = 26 cm

d
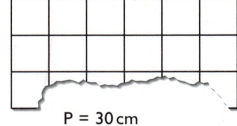
P = 30 cm

e
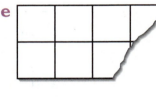
P = 28 cm

f
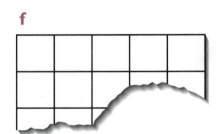
P = 20 cm

2 Find three different ways to complete this rectangle.

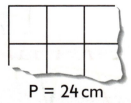
P = 24 cm

3 Construct 5 rectangles each with a perimeter of 22 cm.

4 The perimeter of a rectangle is 60 cm. The shorter side is 9 cm.
What is the length of the longer side?

Refresher

1 Mrs Trayner made this display of photographs of her grandchildren. Calculate the perimeter of each photograph in cm. Show how you worked it out.

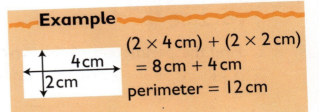

Example

$(2 \times 4\,cm) + (2 \times 2\,cm)$
$= 8\,cm + 4\,cm$
perimeter = 12 cm

4 cm
2 cm

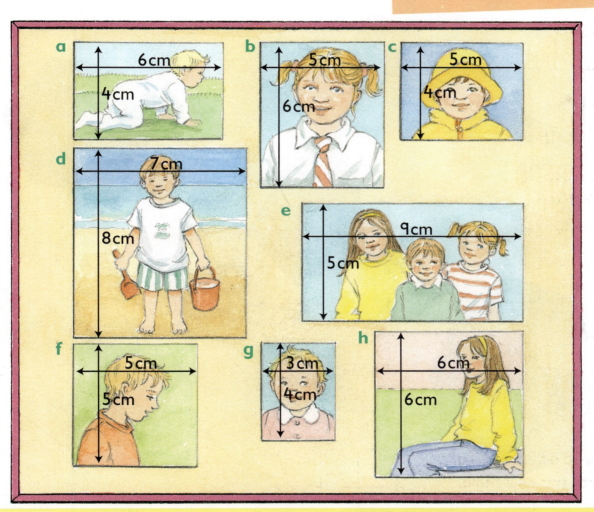

a 6 cm 4 cm
b 5 cm 6 cm
c 5 cm 4 cm
d 7 cm 8 cm
e 9 cm 5 cm
f 5 cm 5 cm
g 3 cm 4 cm
h 6 cm 6 cm

Challenge

You have 9 squares each with sides of 2 cm. What is the largest perimeter you can make? What is the smallest?

Regular perimeters

Practice

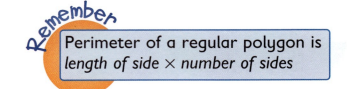

1 a Find the perimeters of these polygons.

b Copy and complete the table.

number of sides of polygon	3	4	5	6	7	8
perimeter in cm						

2 Explain why the perimeter of the hexagon is double that of the triangle.

3 Write what you notice about the perimeters of the square and the octagon.

4 If you continue the pattern, what will the perimeter be for:
a 10-sided regular shape?
a 15-sided regular shape?

Refresher

1 Use your ruler and measure the perimeter of these shapes.

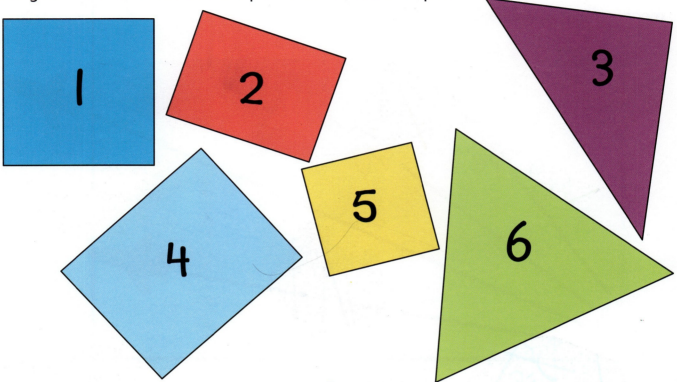

2 Write down the perimeter of each shape.
Show how you worked it out.

3 Which shape has:
  a the largest perimeter
  b the smallest perimeter?

Example

perimeter of shape 1 is:

$$4\,cm + 4\,cm + 4\,cm + 4\,cm = 16\,cm$$

or

$$4 \times 4\,cm = 16\,cm$$

Challenge

These regular hexagons have sides of 1 cm. They make this pattern of shapes.

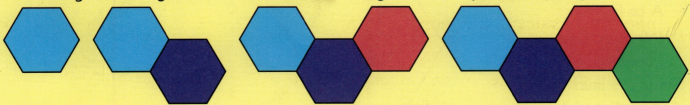

What is the perimeter of the pattern of 10 regular hexagons?

Hint: Draw the first 6 patterns on 1 cm hexagonal grid paper. Then make a table.

83

Measuring in millimetres

Practice

1 Measure these lines to the nearest millimetre. Write each measurement in **3 different ways**.

Example
42 mm = 4 cm 2 mm = 4·2 cm

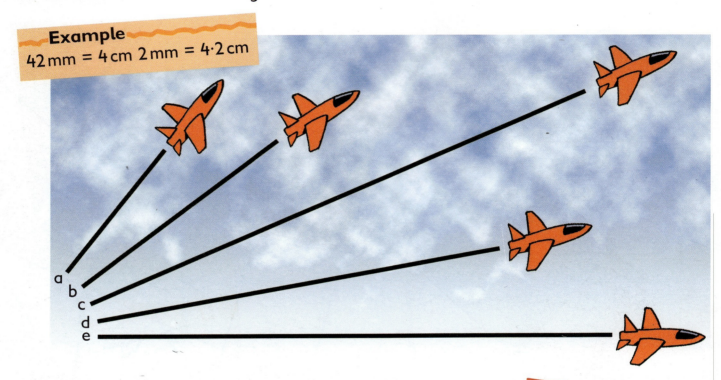

2 Draw lines which are 2·5 cm longer than those in 1a–e.

3 Draw three more zig-zag lines which have a total length of 100 mm.

4 Measure these hexagonal lines to the nearest millimetre.

a A to B

b A to C

c A to D

d A to E

e A to F

f What do you notice about your answers for the lines from A to C and A to E?

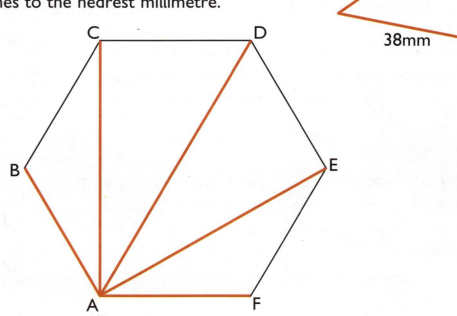

Refresher

1 Measure these lines to the nearest millimetre.
Write your measurements in 3 different ways.

2 Draw lines which are 20 mm longer than the
rods and lines a to f in question 1. Under each
line you draw, write its length in mm.

Example

_____

a = 55 mm

Challenge

1 Construct this rectangular pattern so that each
pair of lines is 5 mm apart. Begin with the smallest
rectangle whose sides are 20 mm and 10 mm.

2 Measure the perimeter of the largest rectangle
in millimetres.

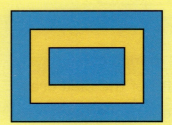

DIY measurements

Practice

1 Write these heights in metres.

  a 420 cm   **b** 800 cm

  c 750 cm   **d** 1500 cm

  e 3800 cm   **e** 6900 cm

2 Write these lengths in millimetres.

  a $\frac{1}{10}$ m   **b** $\frac{3}{10}$ m

  c $\frac{7}{10}$ m   **d** 0·5 m

  e 0·1 m   **f** 0·6 m

3 Tiles are measured in millimetres.
Write these dimensions in centimetres.

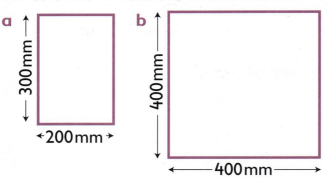

a 300mm × 200mm
b 400mm × 400mm
c 50mm × 250mm

4 Kenny's father is putting tiles above the wash-hand basin in the bathroom.
Each tile is 200 mm wide and 300 mm long.

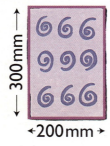

300mm × 200mm

Work out in metres:

a the width of the tiled area

b the height of the tiled area.

86

Refresher

1 Copy and complete these arrow diagrams. The first one is done for you.

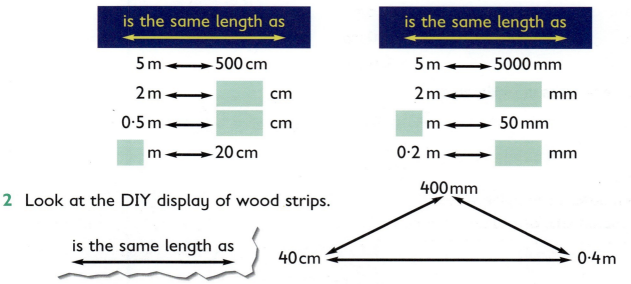

is the same length as		is the same length as
5 m ⟷ 500 cm		5 m ⟷ 5000 mm
2 m ⟷ ☐ cm		2 m ⟷ ☐ mm
0·5 m ⟷ ☐ cm		☐ m ⟷ 50 mm
☐ m ⟷ 20 cm		0·2 m ⟷ ☐ mm

2 Look at the DIY display of wood strips.

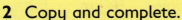

is the same length as

400 mm

40 cm ⟷ 0·4 m

Draw and complete the 3-way relationship for each example.

a	40 cm	b	500 mm	c	0·6 m
d	25 cm	e	900 mm	f	0·8 m

Challenge

1 The DIY store displays this rectangular tiling pattern. Draw the next pattern.

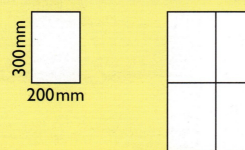

300 mm

200 mm

2 Copy and complete.

pattern number	1	2	3	4
height of pattern in mm				
width of pattern in mm				

3 What if you had 25 tiles? What is the length and breadth you can tile in metres?

Lengths and distances

Example

P = 1·6 m ÷ 4

= 160 cm ÷ 4

= 40 cm

Perimeter = 1·6 m

Practice

1 For each regular polygon, find the length of one side.
Write your answer in cm each time.

a

Perimeter = 2·5 m

b

Perimeter = 0·9 m

c

Perimeter = 4·8 m

d

Perimeter = 5·6 m

2 Fingernails grow about 1 mm each week.
If you never cut your nails,
how long would they be:

a 1 year from now?

b 10 years from now?

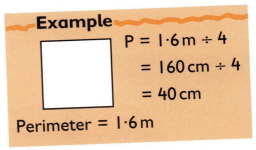

3 a Pat's stride measures about 50 cm.
She lives about 500 m from school.
Approximately how many strides
does she take walking from home
to school?

b A Roman pace is a person's stride
doubled. How many Roman paces does
Pat take for the same distance?

4 Marco is motoring in Italy. He sees this
road sign. About how many miles is it
To Naples? To Pompeii? To Sorrento?

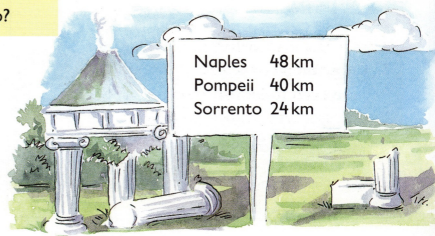

Naples   48 km
Pompeii   40 km
Sorrento 24 km

Refresher

Use this diagram to help you.

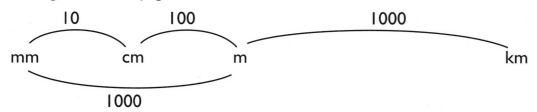

1 Write these sentences choosing the best measurement to make them correct.

a The eraser is about ____ long.   5 mm   55 mm   555 mm

b The fence is about ____ tall.   10 cm   100 cm   1000 cm

c The classroom is about ____ high.   3 m   6 m   12 m

d My uncle is about ____ tall.   1·93 m   19·3 m   193 m

e I live about ____ from school.   2 km   20 km   200 km

2 Three children took part in a sunflower
growing competition.
Here are their results.

Stefan	2000 mm
Seonaid	204 cm
Sheina	2·02 m

Hint. Change all the measurements to millimetres.

Who grew the winning sunflower?
By how many millimetres did it win?

Challenge

Joan is making Christmas decorations.
She needs a piece of ribbon 39 cm long
but she cannot find her measuring tape.
Earlier she cut 3 lengths of ribbon
measuring 31 cm, 33 cm and 37 cm.
Explain how she uses the 3 pieces to
measure the length of ribbon she needs.

Between lengths

Practice

1 Work with a partner. Find 5 objects between 5 cm and 30 cm long.
Record your results like this:

Object	Estimated nearest cm	Measured nearest mm	Converted to cm
paint brush	17 cm	173 mm	17·3 cm

2 Measure each object to the nearest millimetre.

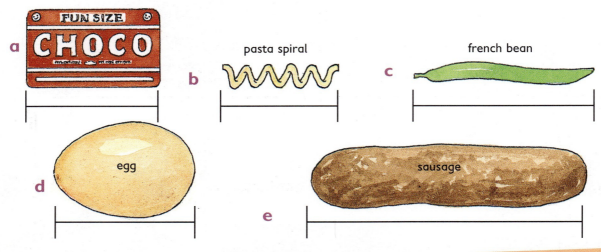

a CHOCO FUN SIZE

b pasta spiral

c french bean

d egg

e sausage

3 For each object in question 2, work out the total length, in
centimetres, of a straight line of 10 identical objects.

4 Work out the length of each key by calculating the distance
between the two arrows. Using decimal notation, record
your answers in centimetres.

> **Example**
> 10 fun-size bars
> total length = 10 × 35 mm
> = 350 mm
> = 35 cm

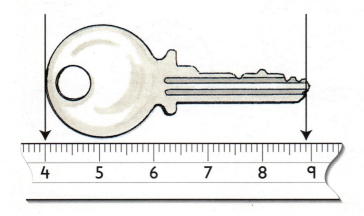

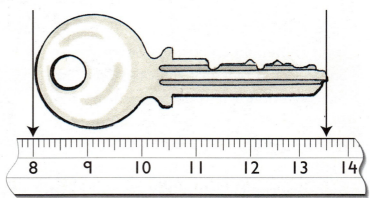

Refresher

1 Estimate and measure these objects to the nearest millimetre.

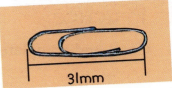

31mm

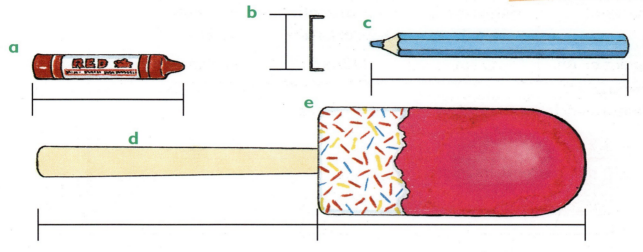

a

b

c

d

e

Example

31 mm = 3·1 cm

2 Now write your answers to question 1 in centimetres.

Challenge

Alison needs four white buttons of the same size for a baby jacket she has knitted. This is her collection of buttons.

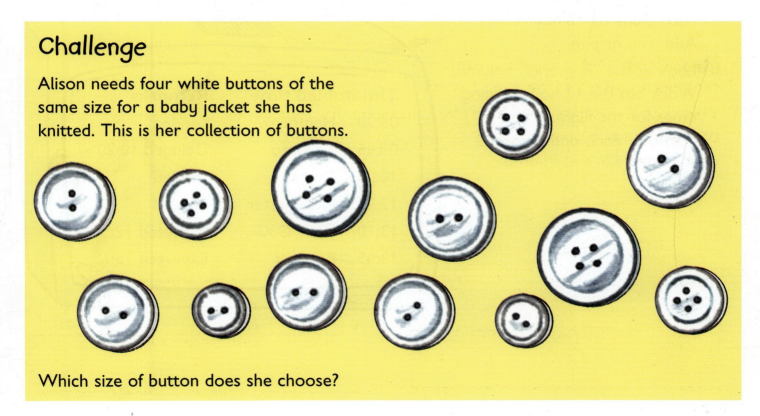

Which size of button does she choose?

24-hour clocks

Practice

Remember

Add 12 to p.m. times to find 24-hour times.

1 Copy and complete this chart.

	Time	12-hour clock	24-hour clock
a	half past 7 in the morning	7:30 a.m.	07:30
b		10:05 a.m.	
c			13:25
d	quarter to 9 in the evening		
e		9:25 p.m.	
f			22:40
g	10 minutes past midnight		
h		2:47 a.m.	
i			20:35

2 Look at the aircraft landing times on the TV monitor.

a Write the timetabled time for each plane as 12-hour times. Add a.m. or p.m.

b Look at the "Remarks" column. Work out the 12-hour landing times for the flights from Toronto, Paris and Brussels.

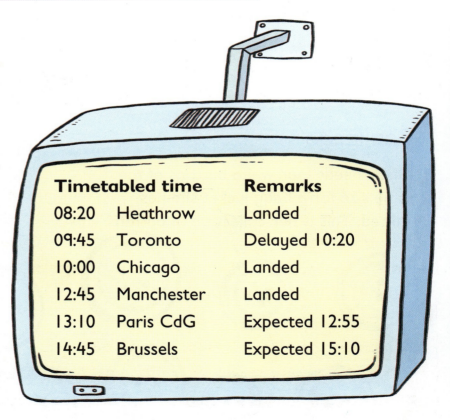

Timetabled time		Remarks
08:20	Heathrow	Landed
09:45	Toronto	Delayed 10:20
10:00	Chicago	Landed
12:45	Manchester	Landed
13:10	Paris CdG	Expected 12:55
14:45	Brussels	Expected 15:10

Refresher

1 Write 24-hour times for:

a

b

c

d quarter past 7 in the morning

e half past 4 in the afternoon

f quarter to 8 in the evening

g 5 minutes to midnight

2 Write 12 hour times for:

a 19:00   **b** 14:15

c 22:30   **d** 15:10

e 18:45   **f** 23:25

Challenge

Ships at sea must have officers on duty at all times. The 24-hour day is divided into watches and the officers take turns to be on duty.

Make up a duty roster for the captain (C), first officer (O) and 3 junior officers (J, K and L).

Example

Time	Watch	Officers
00:00	Middle	O, J
04:00	Morning	

- 2 people on duty at all times.
- No watch should be longer than 6 hours.
- No officer can do more than 12 hours duty in a 24-hour period.
- The captain and first officer are on different watches.

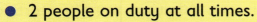

middle watch | morning watch | forenoon watch | afternoon watch | 1st dog watch | 2nd dog watch | first watch

00:00   04:00   08:00   12:00   16:00   20:00   00:00

Calculating times

Practice

Peter is planning his holiday for next year. He makes a list of things he would like to do. He jots down these timings from the holiday brochure.

Activity	Start time	Finish time
Pioneer train trip	11:00	15:30
White water rafting	08:30	13:00
Guided forest hike	10:00	12:15
Hot air ballooning	14:45	17:30
Mountain biking trail	09:00	11:45
Hot springs swimming	16:30	18:30
Lakeside canoeing	13:45	16:15

Use this time line to help you.

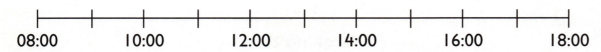

08:00   10:00   12:00   14:00   16:00   18:00

1 Which activity takes the shortest time?

2 Which activity starts at quarter to 2 in the afternoon?

3 Which activity finishes at half past 5 in the evening?

4 List two activities Peter can do on the same day. How long will each activity last?

5 This activity will take four and a half hours to complete. What is it?

6 Lift-off for the hot air balloon is delayed by 35 minutes. What are the new starting and finishing times?

7 After 50 minutes paddling his canoe, Peter stops to take some photographs. What time will his analogue watch show? His camera records the time in the 12-hour clock. What time will be printed on his photographs?

Refresher

Larry's Laundrette

Programme	Wash time	Programme	Drier time
A	60 minutes	1	50 minutes
B	40 minutes	2	30 minutes
C	25 minutes	3	25 minutes

1 For each of these customers:
- work out how long it took to wash and dry clothes
- write the time in 24-hour notation when their laundry was finished

a Mrs Gray arrived at 14:00 used wash programme A and drier programme 2.

b Mr White arrived at 15:15 used wash programme C and drier programme 3.

c Miss Green arrived at 16:50 used wash programme B and drier programme 3.

2 Mrs Brown finished her laundry at 20:30. She used programme C for washing and 1 for drying. At what time on the 12-hour clock did she come into the laundrette?

Challenge

You are cooking a meal for the family. Work out the starting times for the turkey, the potatoes and the vegetables so that the meal is ready to eat at 18:00.

Cooking times

turkey: 6 kg
40 minutes per kg
   + 25 minutes

potatoes: 35 minutes

vegetables: 15 minutes

● Add/subtract any pair of two-digit numbers
● Find a difference by counting up through the next multiple of 10, 100 or 1000
● Partition into H, T and U, adding the most significant digits first

Buzzing calculations

Practice

Remember

Think about the best strategy for each calculation.

l Help the bee get back to his hive by working out the calculations on each flower.

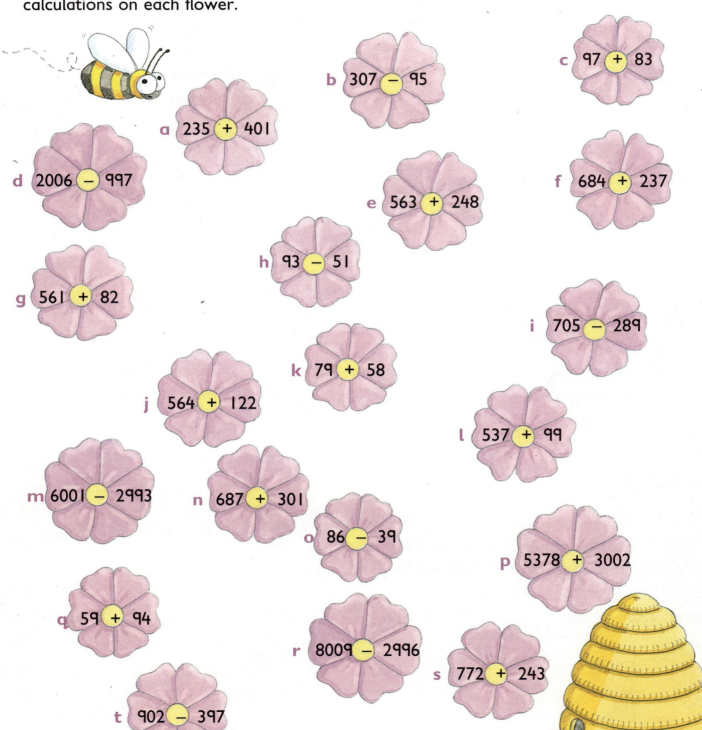

a 235 + 401

b 307 − 95

c 97 + 83

d 2006 − 997

e 563 + 248

f 684 + 237

g 561 + 82

h 93 − 51

i 705 − 289

j 564 + 122

k 79 + 58

l 537 + 99

m 6001 − 2993

n 687 + 301

o 86 − 39

p 5378 + 3002

q 59 + 94

r 8009 − 2996

s 772 + 243

t 902 − 397

Refresher

1 Round each number to the nearest multiple of:

a	10	b	100	c	1000
	61		198		995
	88		304		2996
	37		294		3004
	96		506		4007
	52		399		3992

2 Make an addition and subtraction calculation with each pair of numbers. The first one is done for you.

a

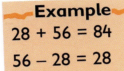

Example
28 + 56 = 84
56 − 28 = 28

b 94 48

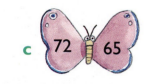

c 72 65

d 87 29

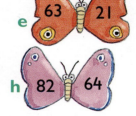

e 63 21

f 54 38

g 74 46

h 82 64

Challenge

1 Use these digits to make up ten addition and subtraction calculations for your friend to work out. Each digit can be used more than once.

 9
 1
 0

Example
6691 + 1969

 6
 5

Write them right!

Practice

Remember
Write the digits in the right columns!

1 Copy out these calculations vertically and then work out the answers.

Example

632 + 571

```
    6 3 2
  + 5 7 1
  1 2 0 3
    1
```

a 542 + 486	b 482 + 735	c 594 + 453	d 681 + 677
e 487 + 745	f 863 + 358	g 293 + 848	h 546 + 876
i 865 + 797	j 734 + 498	k 1647 + 285	l 1459 + 724
m 1683 + 452	n 2827 + 355	o 2508 + 636	p 2482 + 981
q 2673 + 547	r 3865 + 398	s 3962 + 479	t 3783 + 647

Refresher

1 Copy out these calculations vertically and then work out the answers.

Remember
Write the digits in the right columns!

Example
462 + 253

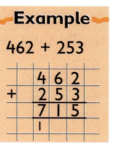

	4	6	2
+	2	5	3
	7	1	5
		1	

a 372 + 464 **b** 328 + 354 **c** 519 + 264 **d** 493 + 251

e 363 + 564 **f** 376 + 218 **g** 456 + 127 **h** 392 + 465

i 483 + 167 **j** 274 + 558 **k** 385 + 624 **l** 197 + 586

Challenge

What to do

Work with a partner.
Take turns to write out a vertical addition calculation.

You need:
● a calculator

1 One person works it out using the written method.
2 The other person checks the answers using the inverse operation – subtraction – on a calculator.
3 Repeat several times swapping roles.

Example
3765 + 896

Work it out!

Practice

Remember

Write the digits in the right columns!

1 Write out these calculations vertically then work out the answers.

a 2678 − 796   b 3462 − 827   c 2503 − 641   d 3261 − 725

e 4572 − 834   f 6525 − 731   g 5230 − 617   h 4327 − 985

i 5032 − 756   j 6246 − 879   k 4973 − 725   l 4036 − 874

2 Now take one number from each tree and make up ten
more subtraction calculations to work out vertically.

a

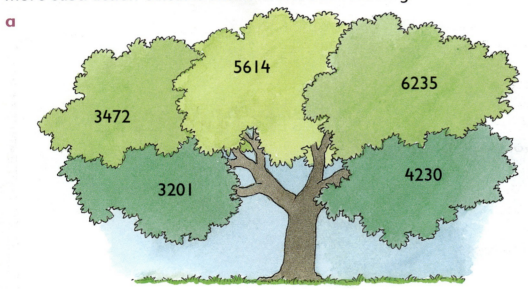

5614   6235   3472   3201   4230

b

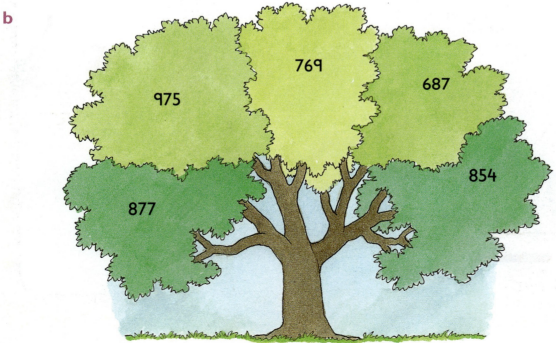

975   769   687   854   877

Refresher

1 Write out these calculations vertically then work out the answers.

a 463 – 247   b 372 – 165   c 416 – 243   d 206 – 152

e 552 – 218   f 494 – 229   g 527 – 173   h 654 – 317

i 416 – 238   j 534 – 295   k 735 – 642   l 495 – 108

Challenge

What to do

Work with a partner.
Take turns to write out a vertical subtraction calculation.

1 One person works it out using the written method.
2 The other person checks the answers using the inverse operation – addition – on a calculator.
3 Repeat several times swapping roles.

You need:
- a calculator

Example
4685 – 973

Problems, problems

Practice

Work out the answers to these problems. Write the calculations you need to work out each problem.

a I have read 196 pages of the 512 pages of my book. How many more pages must I read before I finish my book? How many more pages must I read before I reach the middle of the book?

b I think of a number. I add 74 and then 56. The answer is 197. What was my number? From 197 how many do I need to add to get to 702?

c 7006 people visited the museum last year. So far, 4991 people have visited this year. The museum has predicted that there will be 3020 more visitors this year. What will be the difference between the two years' totals?

d A lorry can hold 205 boxes. The driver has put in 42 boxes at one pick-up and 67 at another. How many more boxes does he have space for? If there were two full lorries how many boxes would they have?

e The total length of the playground is 245 metres. The football area is 75 metres long and the grassy area is 96 metres. What is the length of the rest of the playground?

Refresher

Work out the answers to these problems. Write the calculations you need to work out each problem.

a   Katie has 36 friends and her sister has 47 friends. They want to have a party and invite all their friends. How many invitations do they need?

b   The school kitchen cooked 86 pizzas. 39 got eaten – how many were left?

c   There are 204 people on the train. 98 get off at the first station. How many passengers are left on the train?

d   I think of a number. I add 35 and the answer is 51. What number was I thinking of?

e   145 people have visited the museum so far today. There is a group of 47 children coming this afternoon. What will the total number of visitors be?

Challenge

Make up some word problems about your class and your school. Try to make them two-step problems. Use these calculations.

a $69 - 23 - ? = 12$

b $48 + 96 + ? = 203$

c $712 - 496 - ? = 109$

d $176 + ? + 204 = 478$

And more problems!

Practice

1 Work out these problems using the vertical method.

a I spent £14·26 on some books and £13·87 on a bag. I had £1·13 left. How much money did I have to start with?

b In the first half hour of opening, the sweet shop took £29·86 from customers. £12·73 is given back in change altogether. How much is left in the till?

c I start the day out with £17·39 in my purse. I spend £4·68 on my lunch and I go to the cinema. When I get home I have £8·37 left. How much did the cinema cost?

2 Work out these using a calculator.

a I want to buy five T-shirts since they are on special offer. They are £3·99 each. What change will I get from a £20 note?

b The class has collected £40 towards their outing. The children's tickets will cost £33·47 altogether. Two teachers are going and their tickets cost £1·35 each. How much money will be left?

c I want a coat which is priced at £59·98 and some shoes priced £38·56. The shop reduces everything by half. How much will the two items cost now?

● Choose and use appropriate number operations to solve word problems, and appropriate ways of calculating: mental, mental with jottings, written methods, calculator

Au 11, 5

Refresher

1 Work out these problems using the vertical method.

a I buy two tickets for the match. They cost £12·67 each. How much did I spend?

b I have £17·45 and I spend £8·71 on a present for my mum. How much will I have left?

c I earn £6·78 a week for my Saturday job. How much will I have after three weeks?

d I have saved £12·94 but my sister has saved £5·35 more than me. How much does she have?

e If I spent £4·99 on Monday and £3·42 on Tuesday how much have I spent altogether?

Challenge

1 Which amounts up to £1 cannot be paid exactly with fewer than 6 coins?

88p   98p   89p   99p

Number sequences

Practice

1 Copy and complete the number sequences.

a 1, 7, 13, ⬚, ⬚, ⬚, ⬚, ⬚, ⬚, ⬚

b 2, 11, 20, ⬚, ⬚, ⬚, ⬚, ⬚, ⬚

c −50, ⬚, ⬚, −23, −14, ⬚, ⬚, ⬚

d 60, ⬚, ⬚, ⬚, ⬚, ⬚, 6, −3, −12

e 60, ⬚, ⬚, ⬚, 36, 30, ⬚, ⬚

2 Find your way back to the spaceship by following the correct sequence on the footprints.

Refresher

1 Copy and complete the number sequences.

a 6, 12, 18, ___, ___, ___, ___, ___, ___,

b 9, 18, 27, ___, ___, ___, ___, ___, ___,

c −36, −30, ___, ___, ___, ___, ___, ___,

d −81, ___, ___, ___, ___, −36, ___, ___, −9

2 Add 6 to each of these.

a 42   b 64   c 72   d −12   e −60   f 66

3 Add 9 to each of these.

a 27   b −36   c −54   d 99   e 54   f −90

Challenge

1 Choose a different starting number each time, make 10 jumps.

Jump forwards in:

     a 4s

     b 9s

     c 11s

Jump backwards in:

     d 6s

     e 8s

     f 5s

2 Record each number in sequence.

Square numbers

Practice

1 Write a multiplication fact and a square number fact for each picture.

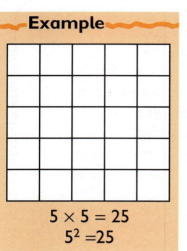

Example

$5 \times 5 = 25$
$5^2 = 25$

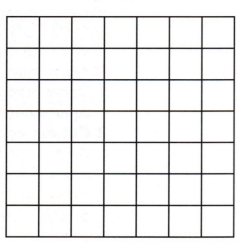

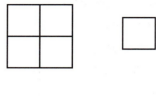

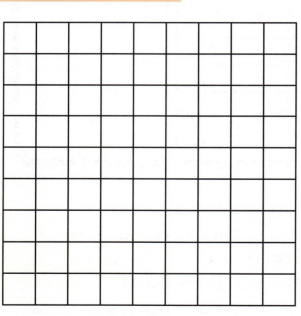

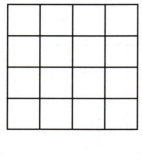

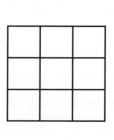

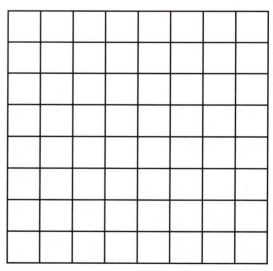

2 Copy and complete.

a ☐² = 64   b ☐ × ☐ = 100   c ☐² = 81

d ☐ × ☐ = 16   e 7 × 7 = ☐   f ☐ × ☐ = 1

g ☐² = 25   h 8 × 8 = ☐   i ☐² = 36

j ☐ × ☐ = 25   k ☐² = 100   l ☐² = 16

m ☐ × ☐ = 4   n 9 × 9 = ☐   o 6 × 6 = ☐

p ☐² = 49   q ☐ × ☐ = 9   r 1² = ☐

Refresher

You need:
- a large sheet of squared paper
- scissors
- a sheet of card

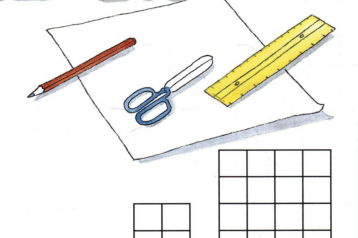

What to do

Work with a partner.
Make a square number display.

1 Draw arrays to make each square number up to 10^2.
2 Cut out each array.
3 Put the arrays in the correct order along a piece of card.
4 Write two number facts for each array, for example $2 \times 2 = 4$
$$2^2 = 4$$

Challenge

$1 \times 1 = 1^2 = 1$ ⟩ $+ 3$
$2 \times 2 = 2^2 = 4$ ⟩ $+ 5$
$3 \times 3 = 3^2 = 9$ ⟩ $+ 7$
$4 \times 4 = 4^2 = 16$

□ × □ = □ = □
□ × □ = □ = □
□ × □ = □ = □
□ × □ = □ = □
□ × □ = □ = □

$10 \times 10 = 10^2 = 100$

1 Write the square numbers and answers in the correct order, one under the other.

2 Look at the answers. Can you see a pattern?

3 Complete the pattern up to 10×10. What is the relationship between square numbers and odd numbers?

4 Use the pattern formed to help find the answers to:
12^2, 17^2, 20^2, 15^2, 13^2.

Finding factors

Practice

1 Fill in the missing **factors**.
Copy and complete.

2 Fill in the missing **products**.
Copy and complete.

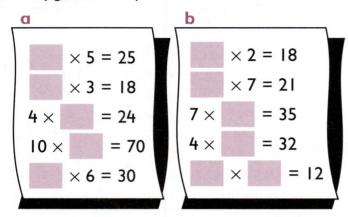

a

$\square \times 5 = 25$

$\square \times 3 = 18$

$4 \times \square = 24$

$10 \times \square = 70$

$\square \times 6 = 30$

b

$\square \times 2 = 18$

$\square \times 7 = 21$

$7 \times \square = 35$

$4 \times \square = 32$

$\square \times \square = 12$

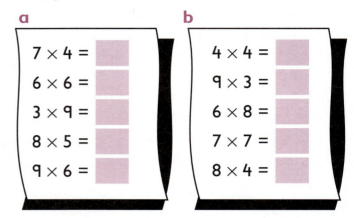

a

$7 \times 4 = \square$

$6 \times 6 = \square$

$3 \times 9 = \square$

$8 \times 5 = \square$

$9 \times 6 = \square$

b

$4 \times 4 = \square$

$9 \times 3 = \square$

$6 \times 8 = \square$

$7 \times 7 = \square$

$8 \times 4 = \square$

3 Write two multiplication number sentences for each set of numbers.
Decide which numbers are the factors and which number is the product.

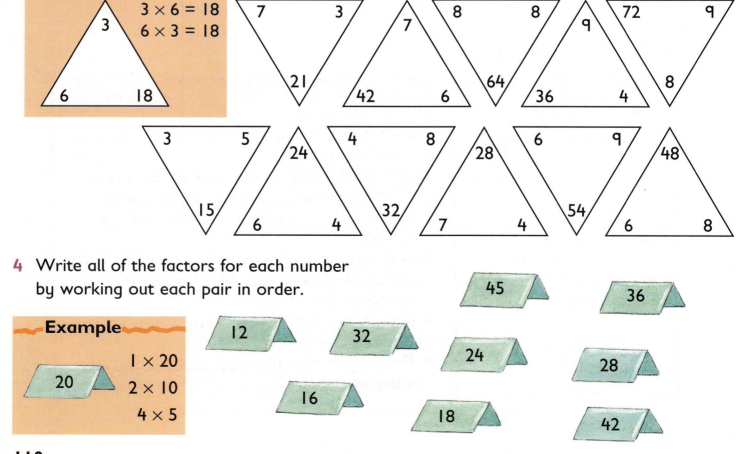

Example

$3 \times 6 = 18$
$6 \times 3 = 18$

3
6   18

7   3
21

3
7
42   6

8   8
64
36

8   9
4
72

72   9
8

3   5
15
6

24
4

4   8
32
7

8
28

6
54

9
6

9
48
8

4 Write all of the factors for each number
by working out each pair in order.

Example

20

1×20
2×10
4×5

12

32

16

45

24

18

36

28

42

Refresher

Example
$4 \times 6 = 24$

You need:
- a pegboard
- 24 pegs

1 How many different ways can you divide 24 pegs to make a square or rectangular shape? Write a multiplication fact for each array shape you make.

2 Use the number of pegs shown to make square or rectangular shapes. Write a multiplication fact for each shape made.

a 16 pegs

b 20 pegs

c 32 pegs

d 36 pegs

e 18 pegs

f 40 pegs

Challenge

Find the factor

You need:

- 2 sets of 1–10 cards

- Number cards 12, 14, 15, 16, 18, 20, 21, 24, 25, 27, 30, 32, 36, 40, 42

What to do

(For 3–4 players)
- Spread out the two sets of 1–10 cards face down on the table.
- Shuffle the other number cards and place them face down in one pile on the table.
- Take turns to select a number card from the pile.
- Turn over one card from the table. If it is a factor, keep the card and select another card from the pile.
- If it is not a factor, replace the card face down on the table.
- The players with the most cards at the end is the winner.

Factor trees

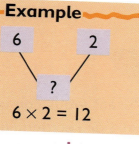

Practice

1 For each set of numbers multiply one number by the other number to find the product.

a 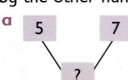 **b** 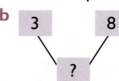 **c** 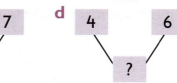 **d**

2 Find the missing factors.

a 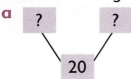 **b** 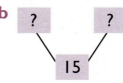 **c** 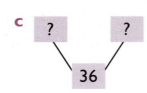 **d**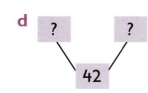

3 Build your own factor trees. Use the numbers below to start. What products can be made?

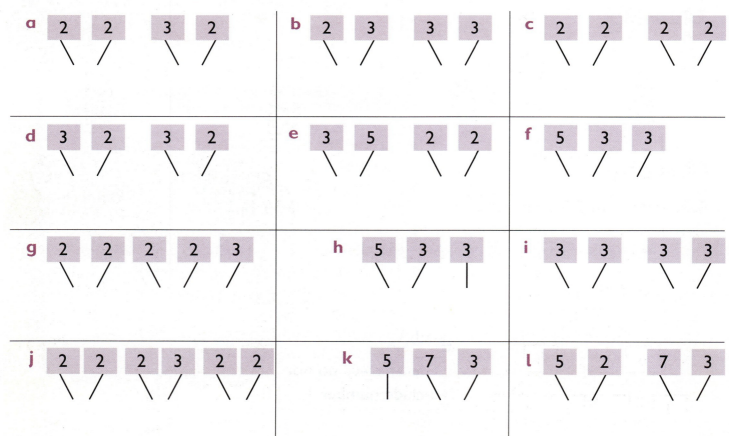

Refresher

Search each tree for all the numbers that are factors of the number on the tree trunk. Write them in the correct pairs. The first one is done for you.

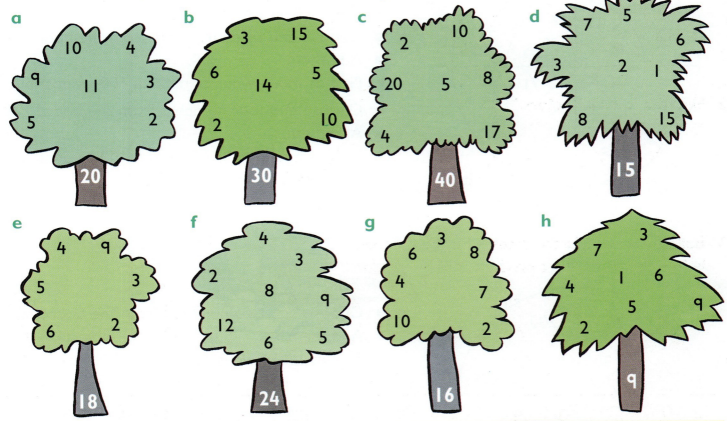

a
10 4
9 11 3
5 2
20

b
3 15
6 5
14
2 10
30

c
2 10
20 5 8
4 17
40

d
7 5
6
3 2 1
8 15
15

e
4 9
5 3
6 2
18

f
4
3
2 8
9
12
6 5
24

g
3 8
6
4 7
10 2
16

h
3
7
4 1 6
5 9
2
9

Challenge

Build your own 5 factor trees.
Choose a number from the apple tree.
Start with the product. What factors can you find?

Example

```
        24
      /    \
    6   ×   4
   / \     / \
  3   2   2   2
```

Remember

Factor trees do not include number 1.

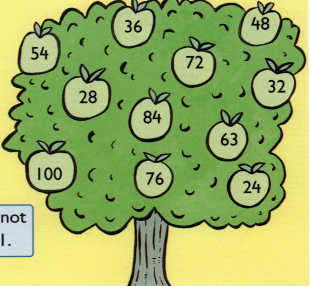

36 48
54 72
28 32
84
63
100 76 24

113

Number puzzles

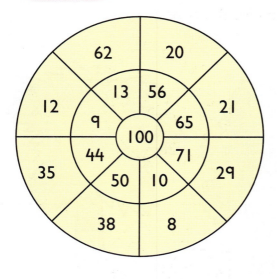

1 Total = 100

a ● Choose any two numbers from the board.
   ● Add them.
   ● Find as many ways of making 100 as possible.

b ● Choose any three numbers from the board.
   ● Add them.
   ● Find as many ways of making 100 as possible.

c ● Choose any four numbers from the board.
   ● Add them.
   ● Find as many ways of making 100 as possible.

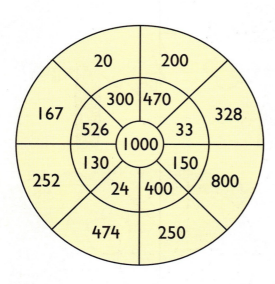

2 Total = 1000

a ● Choose any two numbers from the board.
   ● Add them.
   ● Find as many ways of making 1000 as possible.

b ● Choose any three numbers from the board.
   ● Add them.
   ● Find as many ways of making 1000 as possible.

c ● Choose any four numbers from the board.
   ● Add them.
   ● Find as many ways of making 1000 as possible.

Refresher

1 Find combinations of two numbers on each shape to make the totals shown.

a

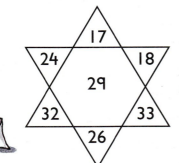

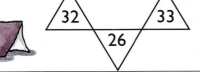

Total = 50

b

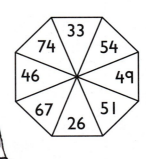

Total = 100

c

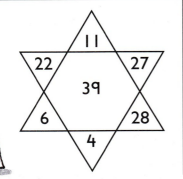

Total = 50

d

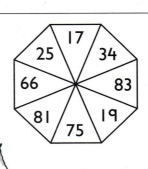

Total = 100

Challenge

1 Double the numbers on the outer ring each time.

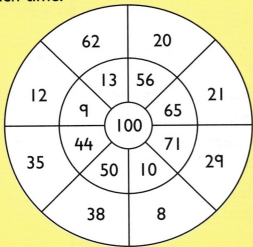

Choose any numbers on the board to find different ways of making 100.

2 Make your own number wheel.

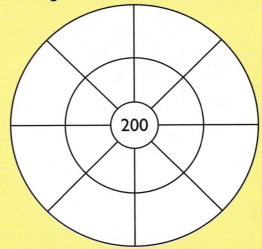

Choose 16 numbers that when added together in combinations of 2, 3 or 4 give the total 200.

Glossary

approximate

Approximate means *nearly* or *round about*. The sign ≈ means *is approximately equal to.*

See also estimate

angles

right angle

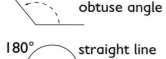

acute angle

obtuse angle

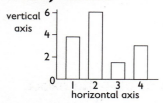

180° straight line

Angles are formed when two straight lines meet. We measure an **angle** by measuring the amount of turn from one line to the other.

Angles are measured in degrees. The symbol for degrees is °.

A right angle is 90 degrees, 90°. A right angle is shown by a small square.

An acute angle is less than 90°.

An obtuse angle is more than 90°.

A straight line has an angle of 180°. This can be used to work out the second angle.

See also protractor

area

Area is the amount of surface of a shape. It is measured in square centimetres. This can be abbreviated to cm².

You can work out the **area** of a rectangle by multiplying the length of the shape by the breadth. Length × breadth = **area**.

ascending

From smallest to largest: **ascending** order.
5   69   235   954   1384

See also descending

axis, axes

vertical axis

horizontal axis

Graphs and charts have two **axes**.

The horizontal **axis** shows the range of data.
The vertical **axis** shows the frequency. They can be labelled in any equal divisions.

See also data

brackets

Brackets are used in maths for grouping parts of calculations together.
10 − (3 + 4) = 7
(10 − 3) + 4 = 11

The calculations in brackets need to be worked out first.

capacity

Capacity is the *amount* that something will hold.
Capacity is measured in litres and millilitres.
1 litre is equal to 1000 millilitres.

Litre can be abbreviated to l.
Millilitres can be abbreviated to ml.

Capacity can also be measured in pints and gallons.

See imperial units

column addition

When you add large numbers, using the standard vertical method can make the calculation easier.

The numbers must be written with the digits of the same place value underneath each other.

If the digits in one column add up to more than 9, the tens are carried to the next column.

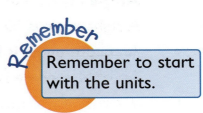

Th	H	T	U
6	9	2	5
+ 2	6	4	8
9	5	7	3
1		1	

Remember

Remember to start with the units.

Hth	Th	H	T	U
2	9	6	8	3
	4	9	7	5
+ 1	6	2	1	3
5	0	8	7	1
2	1	1	1	

◄ You can use this method for more than two numbers.

If you use this method with decimal numbers then the decimal points must be underneath one another.

column subtraction

When you subtract large numbers, using the standard vertical method can make the calculation easier. The numbers must be written with the digits of the same place value underneath each other.

Th	H	T	U
4⁵	⁷7	¹2	5
− 3	8	0	6
1	9	1	9

◄ If the top digit is lower than the bottom digit then 10 can be "borrowed" from the next column.

If you use this method with decimal numbers, then the decimal points must be underneath one another.

consecutive

A **consecutive** number is the *next* number.
The **consecutive** number for 5 is 6.

co-ordinates

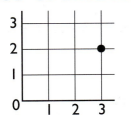

Co-ordinates are numbers or letters that help us to plot the exact position of something. We use them on maps, graphs or charts.

◄ Graphs like this are called the first quadrant.
On the graph, the dot is at (3, 2) 3 lines across and 2 lines up.
To read **co-ordinates** we look *across* and *up*. Some people remember this by thinking of "Along the corridor, up the stairs".

data

Data is information. Interpreting **data** means working out what information is telling you.

A database is a way of storing data. An address book is a data base. A chart is a data base.

decimals

Decimal fractions show us the part of a number that is not a whole number.

H	T	U	.	ths	hdths
		5	.	8	
		5	.	8	6

The decimal point separates the whole numbers from the decimal fractions.

◄ Each digit after the decimal point has a different place value.

5·8 is a number with one decimal place.
5·86 is a number with two decimal places.

Ordering decimals

We **order** decimal numbers by comparing the digits, starting from the left, as this is the highest value digit. If these two digits are the same then we compare the next two digits, and so on.

```
                              These 3 digits are the same.
41·8⑤
41·8⑨                         We compare these 2 digits to order these numbers.
```

Rounding decimals

To round a decimal to the to the nearest whole number, we look at the tenths digit. If the digit is 5 or more, we round the number *up* to the next whole number. If the digit is less than 5, we round the number *down* to the next whole number.

8.26 will be rounded down to 8 to make 8.1
8.59 will be rounded up to 9 to make 8.7

Decimals and fractions

All decimals have a fraction equivalent. To find the decimal equivalent for a fraction we divide 1 by the denominator and then multiply by the numerator.

$\frac{3}{4}$ = 0·75
1 ÷ **4** = 0·25
0·25 x **3** = 0·75

$\frac{1}{2}$ = 0·5
$\frac{1}{4}$ = 0·25
$\frac{3}{4}$ = 0·75
$\frac{1}{10}$ = 0·1
$\frac{3}{10}$ = 0·3
$\frac{1}{5}$ = 0·2
$\frac{1}{100}$ = 0·01
$\frac{3}{100}$ = 0·03

See *also* fractions

descending

From largest to smallest: **descending** order.
1384   954   235   69   5

See *also* ascending

difference

When finding the **difference** between numbers, we find how many *more* or *less* one number is than another.

digit

Numbers are made up of **digits**.

        5 is a single-or one-digit number
       23 is a two-digit number
      147 is a three-digit number
     2082 is a four-digit number
    63 581 is a five-digit number
   987 206 is a six-digit number

Each **digit** in a number represents a different value.

See also place value

divisibility

There are some quick tests you can do to see if one number will divide by another.

You can use your knowledge of multiplication facts: $3 \times 4 = 12$ so 12 is divisible by 3 and 4.

Other tests:

2s   Any even number is divisible by 2.

4s   If you can divide the last two digits of the number by 4 exactly, the whole number will divide exactly by 4. 216 is divisible by 4 as 16 is divisible by 4.

5s   You can divide 5 exactly into any number ending in 5 or 0.

10s   If a number ends in 0 you can divided it by 10 exactly.

100s   If a number ends in two zeros it will divide exactly by 100.

dividing by 10 and 100

When a number is **divided by 10** the digits move one place value to the right. If the units digit is zero it disappears, if it is not zero it becomes a decimal tenth.

The place value of the digits decrease 10 times.

When a number is **divided by 100** the digits move two place values to the right. If the tens and units digits are zero they disappear, if not they become decimals, hundredths and tenths.

The place value of the digits decreases 100 times.

See also multiplying by 10 and 100

division facts

Division facts are the all the division calculations that correspo the multiplication facts.

$4 \times 5 = 20$
$20 \div 5 = 4$

See also multiplication facts

equivalent fractions

Equivalent fractions are fractions of equal value. They are worth the same.

$\frac{4}{8}$ is equivalent to $\frac{1}{2}$

Equivalent fractions can be worked out by multiplying the numerator and the denominator by the same number.

$$\frac{1 \times 2}{2 \times 2} = \frac{2 \times 2}{4 \times 2} = \frac{4 \times 2}{8 \times 2} = \frac{8 \times 2}{16 \times 2} = \frac{16}{32}$$

Or by dividing the numerator and the denominator by the same number.

See also fractions

estimate

An **estimate** is a sensible guess.

1997 + 2109. The answer is approximately 4000.

See also approximate

factor

A **factor** is a whole number which will divide exactly into another whole number.

The factors of 12 are 1, 2, 3, 4, 6, 12 as they all divide into 12.

The factors can be put into pairs. If the pairs are multiplied together they will equal 12.

1 × 12
2 × 6
3 × 4

figures

A whole number can be written in **figures**: 485
or in **words**: four hundred and eighty five

formula

A **formula** is a way of writing down a rule.

For example, to find the area of a rectangle you multiply the length by the width.

fractions

Fractions are parts of something.

$\frac{1}{2}$ → numerator
→ denominator

The numerator tells you how many parts we are talking about.
The denominator tells you how many parts the whole has been split into.

We find fractions of amounts by dividing by the denominator and then multiplying by the numerator.

We divide by the denominator as this is the number of parts the amount needs to be divided into. We then multiply by the numerator as this is the number of parts we are talking about.

See also fractions

halving

To **halve** a number you divide it by 2.
Half 12 = 6
$12 \div 2 = 6$

Doubling and halving are inverse operations.

See also inverse operations

imperial units

These used to be the standard measurements in Britain. They have now been replaced by metric units. Some imperial units are still used today.

Capacity
Pints and gallons
8 pints = 1 gallon

Length
Miles
1 mile = 1·6 km

improper fractions

An **improper fraction** is a fraction where the numerator is more than the denominator.

$\frac{13}{5}$

These are sometimes called top heavy fractions.
Improper fractions can be changed to whole numbers or mixed numbers.

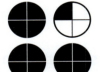

◄ $\frac{5}{4} = 1\frac{1}{4}$

◄ $\frac{8}{4} = 2$

A fraction that is not an **improper fraction** is a proper fraction.

See also fractions
See also mixed numbers

integer

Integer is another name for a whole number.

See also whole number

inverse operations

Inverse means *the opposite operation*. The **inverse operation** will undo the first operation.

Addition and subtraction are **inverse operations**:
17 + 26 = 43   43 − 26 = 17

Multiplication and division are **inverse operations**:
$6 \times 9 = 54$ $54 \div 9 = 6$

length

Length is how long an object or a distance is.
Length is measured in kilometres, metres, centimetres and millimetres.

1 kilometre is equal to 1000 metres.
1 metre is equal to 100 centimetres.
1 centimetre is equal to 10 millimetres.

Kilometre can be abbreviated to km.
Metre can be abbreviated to m.
Centimetre can be abbreviated to cm.
Millimetre can be abbreviated to mm.

Length can also be measured in miles.

See *also* imperial units

long multiplication

```
    3 5 2
×     2 7
  7 0 4 0
  2 4 6 4
  9 5 0 4
      1
```

When you multiply numbers which are too large to work out mentally, you can use **long multiplication**. We call it **long multiplication** when both numbers involved are more than a single-digit.

The numbers must be written with the digits of the same place value underneath each other.

See *also* short multiplication

mass

Mass is another word for weight.
Mass is measured in grams and kilograms.
1 kilogram is equal to 1000 grams.

mixed number

A **mixed number** is a number that has a whole number and a fraction.

$2\frac{1}{4}$ $5\frac{1}{2}$ $7\frac{3}{8}$

See *also* fractions

mode

The **mode** of a set of data is the number that occurs most often.

multiplication

Multiplication is the inverse operation to division.
Numbers can be multiplied in any order and the answer will be the same.
$5 \times 9 = 45$ $9 \times 5 = 45$

See *also* inverse operations

multiplying by 10 and 100

Th	H	T	U
		2	3
	2	3	0

$23 \times 10 = 230$

Our number system is based around 10.
When a number is **multiplied by 10** the digits move one place value to the left and zero goes in the empty column to keep its place value.

◀ The place value of the digits increases 10 times.

When a number is **multiplied by 100** the digits move two place values to the left and zeros go in the empty columns to keep their place value.

The place value of the digits increases 100 times.

See *also* dividing by 10 and 100

multiplication facts to 10×10

Multiplication facts are the multiplication calculations from all the tables to 10.

See *also* division facts

multiples	A **multiple** is a number that can be divided into another number.

A **multiple** is a number that can be divided into another number.

2, 4, 6, 8, 10, 12 are all **multiples** of 2 as we can divide 2 into them all.

10, 20, 30, 40, 50, 60, 70 are all **multiples** of 10 as we can divide 10 into them all.

Multiples can be recognised by using the multiplication facts.

See also multiplication facts

negative numbers

Numbers and integers can be positive or **negative**.
Negative integers or numbers are *below* zero.

Negative numbers have a minus sign before them.
−56

Negative numbers are ordered in the same way as positive numbers except they run from right to left.

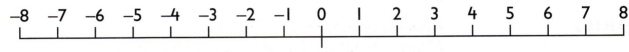

See also positive numbers

net

A **net** is a flat shape which can be cut out and folded up to make a solid shape.

<, >, <, >

are symbols used to order numbers.

< means less than   45<73
> means more than   73>45
< means less than or equal to   45<45, 44
> means more than or equal to 87>87, 88

ordering fractions

When you **order fractions** and mixed numbers, first look at the whole numbers then the fractions. If the fractions have different denominators, think about the fractions in relation to a half to help you to order them.

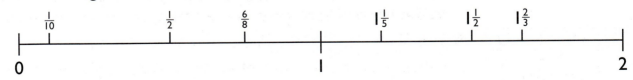

ordinal

Ordinal numbers show the place of ordered items.

First, second, third, fourth, fifth, sixth, seventh, eighth, ninth, tenth …
1st, 2nd, 3rd, 4th, 5th, 6th, 7th, 8th, 9th, 10th …

parallel

Parallel lines are lines that are the same distance apart all the way along.

◀ They are often shown by two little arrows.

percentage

The sign % stands for per cent, which means out of 100. 30% means 30 out of 100.

Percentages are linked to fractions and decimals.

$\frac{1}{2} = 50\% = 0.5$

$\frac{1}{4} = 25\% = 0.25$

$\frac{3}{4} = 75\% = 0.75$

$\frac{1}{5} = 20\% = 0.2$

$\frac{1}{10} = 10\% = 0.10$

Finding percentages of amounts

To find **percentages** of amounts we need to use the relationship to fractions.

To find 50% of an amount, we divide by 2: $50\% = \frac{1}{2}$. 50% of £40 is £20.

To find 25% we divide by 4: $25\% = \frac{1}{4}$
To find 20% we divide by 5: $20\% = \frac{1}{5}$

perpendicular

A **perpendicular** line meets another line at right angles.

perimeter

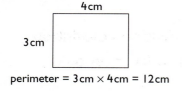

4 cm
3 cm

perimeter = 3 cm × 4 cm = 12 cm

Perimeter is the distance all the way around a flat shape.

You can calculate the **perimeter** of a shape by adding the length of all the sides together.

If a shape has sides all the same length then you can use multiplication to work out the **perimeter**.

place value

The **place value** of a digit is what it is *worth*.

In **467** the **place value** of the 6 is 60 or 6 tens.
In **624** the **place value** of the 6 is 600 or 6 hundreds.

See also digit

positive numbers

Numbers and integers can be **positive** or negative.

Positive numbers or integers are above zero. They can be written with a + sign before them. If there is no sign before a number it is always counted as positive.

See also negative numbers

probability

Probability is about how *likely* or *unlikely* the outcome of an event is. The event maybe the throw of a die or whether or not it will rain today.

We use certain words to discuss **probability**. We can put events and the words on a scale from *no chance of it happening* to *certain*.

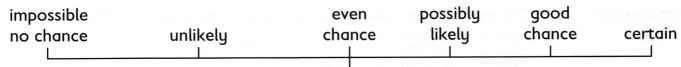

| impossible no chance | | unlikely | | even chance | | possibly likely | | good chance | | certain |

Even chance means an event is as likely to happen as not happen.

product

Product is another name for the answer to a multiplication calculation.

24 is the product of 6 × 4

proportion

Proportion shows the relationship between two connected things.

When amounts are being compared and they have equal ratios they are in **proportion**.

1 packet of biscuits costs 60p
2 packets of biscuits cost £1·20
3 packets cost £1·80
The cost is in **proportion** to the number of packets bought.

See *also* ratio

protractor

A **protractor** is used to draw and measure angles. **Protractors** can be circular or semi-circular.

quotient

Quotient is another name for the answer to a division calculation.

The remainder of the **quotient** can be shown as a fraction or a decimal fraction.

$27 \div 4 = 6 \text{ r } 3$
$27 \div 4 = 6\frac{3}{4}$
$27 \div 4 = 6 \cdot 75$

As we are dividing by 4, the fraction will be a quarter and there are 3 of them left. 0·75 is the decimal equivalent to $\frac{3}{4}$.

range

The **range** of a set of data is the lowest to the highest value.

ratio

Ratio is a way of comparing amounts or numbers.

It can be used in two ways:

It can describe the relationship between *part to whole*.
A cake is divided into 4 equal parts and one part is eaten. The **ratio** of part to whole is one part in every four parts or 1 in 4.

Or it can describe the relationship of *part to other part*.
A cake is divided into 4 parts and one part is eaten. The ratio of part to part is 1 to 3 as for every piece eaten three pieces are left.

The **ratio** 1 to 3 can also be written as 1:3.

See *also* proportion

reflection

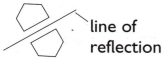

line of reflection

◄ If a shape is **reflected**, it is drawn as it would appear reflected in a mirror held against or alongside one of its sides.

reflective symmetry

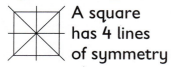

A square has 4 lines of symmetry

A shape is symmetrical if both sides are the same when a line is drawn through the shape. The line can be called a mirror line or an axes.

◄ Some shapes have more than one line of symmetry.

rounding

To **round** a number *to the nearest* 10, we look at the units digit.

If it is 5 or greater, we round the it up to the next 10. **345** rounds up to 350

If it is less than 5, we round it down to the previous 10. **343** rounds down to 340

To **round** a number *to the nearest* 100, we look at the tens digit.

If it is 5 or greater, we round it up to the next 100. **462** rounds up to 500

If it is less than 5, we round it down to the previous 100. **437** rounds down to 400

To **round** a number to the nearest 1000, we look at the hundreds digit.

If it is 5 or greater, we round it up to the next 1000. **2768** rounds up to 3000

If it is less than 5, we round it down to the previous 1000. **2469** rounds down to 2000

scales

Scales are used on measuring equipment. Not all divisions are labelled, so to read a scale accurately you need to work out what each division represents. This varies from scale to scale.

short division

When you divide numbers that are too large to work out mentally, you can use **short division**. We call it **short division** when one of the numbers involved is a single-digit.

short multiplication

	3	4	6
×			9
3	1	1	4
		4	5

When you multiply numbers that are too large to work mentally, you can use **short multiplication**. We call it **short multiplication** when one of the numbers involved is a single-digit.

◄ The numbers must be written with the digits of the same place value underneath each other.

See also long multiplication

square numbers

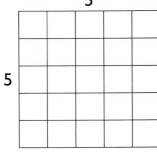

5

5

To **square** a number it is multiplied by itself. The answer is a **square number**.

To square 5, we multiply 5 by itself. 25 is the **square number**.

◄ $5 \times 5 = 25$ can also be written as $5^2 = 25$

Square numbers have an odd number of factors. The factors of 25 are 1, 5, 25.

Square numbers up to 100

$1 \times 1 = 1$
$2 \times 2 = 4$
$3 \times 3 = 9$
$4 \times 4 = 16$
$5 \times 5 = 25$
$6 \times 6 = 36$
$7 \times 7 = 49$
$8 \times 8 = 64$
$9 \times 9 = 81$
$10 \times 10 = 100$

See *also* factor

symmetrical pattern

Patterns can be **symmetrical**. They may have two lines of symmetry.

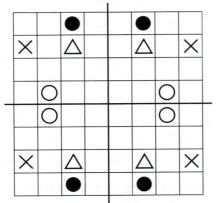

line of symmetry

line of symmetry

time

These are the units **time** is measured in:
seconds
minutes
hours
days
weeks
months
years

These are the relationships between these units:

60 seconds = 1 minute
60 minutes = 1 hour
24 hours = 1 day
7 days = 1 week
4 weeks = 1 month
12 months = 1 year
365 days = 1 year

analogue
clock

digital
clock

◄ **Time** can be read on analogue clocks or digital clocks.

Digital clocks can be 12 hour or 24 hour.
The 12-hour clock uses a.m. and p.m.
The 24-hour clock carries on after 12 o'clock midday to 24 instead of starting at 1 again.

translation

A **translation** is when a shape is moved by sliding it.

triangles

A **triangle** is a 2D shape with three straight sides and three angles.

There are four kinds of triangle:

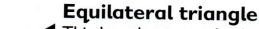

Equilateral triangle
◄ This has three equal sides and three equal angles.

Isosceles triangle

◄ This has two equal sides. The angles opposite these two sides are also equal.

Scalene triangle

◄ All three sides are different lengths.
The angles are all different too.

Right-angled triangle
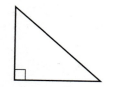
◄ This has one right angle.

whole number

A **whole number** is a number without decimals or fractions.
See also integer